COVID-1984

How the States of the World Destroyed Liberty

George Beglan

COVID-1984 : How the States of the World Destroyed Liberty

Print ISBN 978-1-949267-75-4
ebook ISBN 978-1-949267-76-1

Cover Design by Guy Corp
www.grafixcorp.com

STAIRWAY PRESS—Apache Junction

STAIRWAY≡PRESS

www.StairwayPress.com
1000 West Apache Trail, Suite 126
Apache Junction, AZ 85120

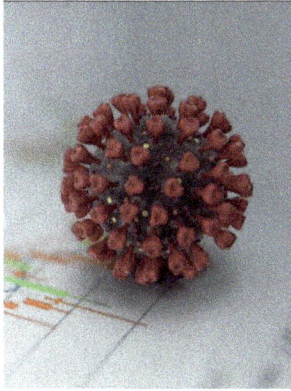

Publisher's Note

WE SURVIVED AN odd period of modern history—and, in my opinion—a transitional one. In a two-year virus cycle, something like 650,000 people in the United States died with or from COVID (SARS-CoV-2) and our lives changed forever.

Artificial Intelligence and social media giants pushed and prodded and watched the results with extreme focus. Faceless, unelected mini-dictators popped up everywhere and got media exposure while indulging their burning desire to rule—with directives, mandates, dictates and lockdowns.

But, will we ever know the true origination of this disease? Was it a natural variant or a lab experiment gone wrong? Or, was it a perfectly executed culling of the old, obese and sick?

Will we ever have accurate, reliable counts of cases and deaths? Will we ever know if there are intelligent ways to avoid the virus, prepare our immune systems to deal with inevitable exposure or cure the disease once it takes hold?

One of the problems with our modern age of big data—beyond inevitable propaganda pollution, gaslighting, provocateur-bots and false flag operations—is that no matter what or who you chose to believe; you will find commentary, studies, white papers, articles and tortured facts to justify your opinion and feed your confirmation bias.

I wish good fortune to those trying to intelligently navigate all of this.

It's possible experimental, therapeutic mRNA treatments are a pivotal advance in human health. It's also possible this technology has long-term effects or unintended consequences and will be a complete, Thalidomide-level disaster.

Only time will tell.

> Recognizing the broad potential of mRNA science, we set out to create an mRNA technology platform that functions very much like an operating system on a computer. It is designed so that it can plug and play interchangeably with different programs. In our case, the 'program' or 'app' is our mRNA drug—the unique mRNA sequence that codes for a protein.[i]

In all of this confusion, there is one thing certain: as annotated here in George's book, the unholy (and temporary, I hope) alliance of the tyrannical, bureaucratic state and social media giants will take advantage of any situation to increase their monopoly powers and control.

The results of the pandemic were not all bad. I enjoy web conferencing technology that enables working from home. No business travel for 18 months was more relief than burden. And, maybe there *are* too many of us with freedom to travel around the world. There certainly are hazards related to immigration, business and leisure travel. Clearly, the elite powers did not like the human herd's freedom of movement and our large gatherings like church services, rock concerts and sporting events.

But, how do we weigh the hazards against the joys of liberty?

What we do is worth risk.

Do we want bureaucrats weighing the costs and benefits—then dictating how we should live our lives?

I don't.

---

[i] https://www.modernatx.com/mrna-technology/mrna-platform-enabling-drug-discovery-development

Contents

About the Author

George is the former president of the Oxford Hayek Society. This is his first book.

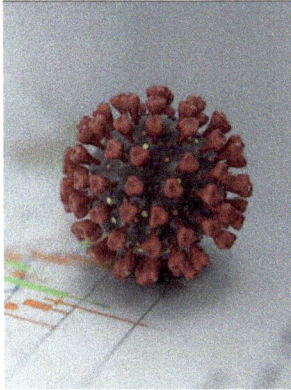

Foreword

THE CORONAVIRUS, COVID-19, or SARS-COV-2, has redefined civil liberties and rights as we know them. In response to the emergence of this pandemic, nations all around the world—bar few—have seen fit to strip away the liberties and rights of their peoples.

The object of this book is to expose that policy for the disastrous miscalculation it is in consequential terms and its moral illegitimacy in deontological terms through a series of comparative matrices provided by the varying policies of nations around the world.

Some argue this is justified with this specific crisis as one does not inherently know whether or not one has passed on the virus until it is too late. We argue in counter that actions taken by governments in the form of national lockdowns, amongst other actions, when stripped of euphemism, resemble the moral valence of actions they would take against violent criminals, for example, lockdown is comparably valent to house arrest.

It is therefore especially crucial in such circumstances that we not discard the *mens rea* element associated with such actions and treat all people's actions as equivalent without intention for precisely that reason; they may well not know they act as vectors for the virus, if at all.

Reacting to the emergence of this virus with a fear-induced miasma of panic in the halls of governance, resulting in turn in the blatant violations of civil liberties which have occurred throughout the last year and which will likely continue into the future, should show the true nature of government to all who have been affected by the policies in question, irrespective of how they are spun.

That brings us neatly onto the next point and recurring theme throughout the last year.

Many negative effects associated with government actions (crashing economies, attempting to recover by printing huge amounts of money and thereby creating debt on people-to-come who were never given the opportunity to consent to it (or not), and lockdown-induced deaths, amongst others) have been spun as consequences of the virus itself, rather than the associated government actions.

This corruption of causality has been aided and abetted by many media outlets playing along with the collective delusion. Whilst it may be true to suggest that governments would not have taken these actions if not for the virus, the fact that governments took them provides the closer causal link and is thereby the prime factor; if one wanted to sincerely argue that the virus, rather than government action, was responsible for the long-term economic catastrophes and malaises which will follow this year, one would have to submit, somehow in a logically consistent way, that the virus started up the money printers and morphed into something barring people's doors shut, more than government actions taken in response to it.

A patently absurd suggestion once expressed explicitly.

The overriding point of course, is that the safeguards of civil liberties have failed. Their very point is to safeguard the rights of people irrespective of circumstances and how governments hijack them to induce whatever actions they find appropriate at the time.

The history of previous 'national lockdowns' around the world being congregated almost entirely in either totalitarian states or those with forms of governments which disregard civil liberties through their forms of governance should in and of itself be an indication, especially to those statists primed to make nonarguments to the provenance of a policy or individual in other areas, such as the arguments we saw being mounted by BLM protestors in the U.S. to tear down the statutes of American founding fathers—their provenance as slaveholders was corrupt and so they should not be allowed to stand in the modern day.

Such nonarguments and appeals to faux logic were notably absent when discussing lockdown policies...

Coming from that example to the conclusion of my section of the foreword, I am reminded of U.S. Founding Father Benjamin Franklin's immortal words on two occasions.

I address the first, from the 11th of November 1755, to the citizen-reader of this book:

> *Those who would give up essential Liberty, to purchase a little temporary Safety, deserve neither Liberty nor Safety.*

The second, I address, in no matter what futility, to the 'leaders', governors and administrators throughout the world, from 1738:

> *Sell not virtue to purchase wealth, nor Liberty to purchase power.*

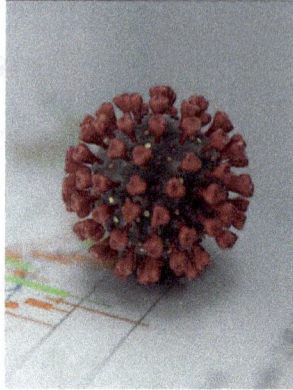

Section 1—Viewpoints, Arguments and Cases in Abstract

Voluntaryism is the radical idea that you belong to yourself.
—Unknown

The Author's Viewpoint and Method This Book Takes

IT WILL DO well to state at the outset that the author is a voluntarist, and to briefly summarise this position.

Some may be acquainted with the political-economic praxis which most voluntarists hold and reversely acquainted with the philosophy through it: Anarcho-Capitalism, a position where theories of anarchy and capitalism intersect, as described by Rothbard, Mises, David D. Friedman and Block amongst others; one should refer to their works for theoretical models of greater detail.

Tautologising their work would both be a disservice and outside the bounds of this book. Furthermore, the author is somewhat more open to left-libertarian positions and traditions than those positions and scholars alone might seem to indicate, at least, those elements also willing to work with us.

I have found those that are willing to do so are some of the hardest working people, possessed of some of the best character around.

The philosophical view, separate from economics, holds that all transactions between people must be wholly voluntary throughout the entirety of their duration in order to morally stand.

This is derived on the grounds of our self-ownership, which is self-evident, and therefore our ownership over our own agency, and therefore, our own actions. It is arguable that all of Western Liberalism since the Enlightenment follows this train of thought; echoes of it are reflected in the U.S. Constitution, The Gettysburg Address and elsewhere.

We submit that only voluntarists, no matter their preferred economic model, uphold and practice this revelation, and its implications on policy, praxis and ultimately, individual behaviour, consistently.

I will outwardly and earnestly dispense with the greatest deterrent to most people. This point of view leads to the conclusion that states, at least as they exist, self-define and propagate as self-enforcing monopolists on the market for organised violence, are ethically bankrupt institutions, from beginning to end.

It is worth distinguishing these mechanisms of social management from ideas of nation, more tied to community. Whilst membership of a nation may be arbitrary as one cannot choose one's mother, nor her nationality, the distinction must be acknowledged; we are not intent on abolishing any pride the dear reader may have in their forebears.

On this, consistency, which can usually be de-euphemised to simple honesty, demands there be no compromise. This insistence is what distinguishes voluntarists from other species of liberal. If you find this position at least understandable, rational to any degree or are open to being convinced of this view, at least in application to and through the matrix of the COVID-19 pandemic, then read on. If this has closed your mind to the contents of this book, please gift it to someone who you think will derive greater profit from it and read no further.

Astute readers may notice this as a useful epistemic tool; to see the illegitimacy of the actions taken by many states, as well as globalist and supranational institutions, both within and without this COVID-19 pandemic as context, strip away euphemisms.

Think plainly of the actions of one's state or government as if they were one's own. Governments are made up of people and it would be logically illiterate exceptionalism, as well as a remarkably dangerous rule, to claim one rule for those constituting their ranks and another for their subjects.

Generally, let 'war' become 'state-sponsored mass murder', 'taxation' become 'robbery' (theft may be the phrase with the better ring to it but fails to communicate the inherently violent element in my view) and 'licensing' become 'racketeering'.

You get the pattern.

For the context of the COVID-19 pandemic specifically, let 'lockdown' become 'house arrest', 'mandatory social distancing' become 'violation of the right to free association' and the threat, though yet to manifest (at least publicly) but concept discussed in the public consciousness of 'mandatory medical treatment' become 'violation of the right to bodily autonomy'.

On the subject of epistemic tools, readers familiar with Bayesian rationalism may notice an attempt at invoking its presence in these pages.

This is intentional.

The pandemic this book discusses is subject to the scientific method; so therefore, should be any discussion surrounding it, no matter if that discussion falls more within the bounds of philosophy, politics and economics than biology. I find no epistemic method or point-of-view better for this purpose than that espoused by Rationalists, and also recommend all their works to you.

There will be no discussion or invocation of theology and the exceptions to that method it might invoke; within the set of actions which are deontologically permitted, probabilistic discernment, based on Bayesian reasoning, is the best epistemic tool for determining which methods, in service of corresponding goals, best consequentially justify themselves.

The tension between the claim normally used by those who work *a priori* to determine truth absolutely and the rationalist idea of subjective probability acting as a refutation of such an idea is acknowledged.

My own mind is not yet made up on this tension, if it is an irreconcilable one at all, which does not seem obvious, and further discussion would likely be outside the bounds of this book.

Hence, the moral process of this book and author is set out: initial voluntarist views define the set of acceptable solutions deontologically, and then one distinguishes between them on which is most likely to produce the most utility using the methods of Rationalists, subject to any weighting one finds necessary, i.e., consequentially.

Applying the Voluntarist Viewpoint to the COVID-19 Pandemic and Resulting Arguments

It will do well in the first chapter to state arguments to be applied throughout the book across examples in brief. There may be additional commentary on them where appropriate in each example but it would be tautologous to repeat the arguments over and over across differing exhibits with the same core logic.

The first argument to be addressed is chiefly that which states that national lockdowns and/or stay-at-home orders are intolerable violations of the natural and self-evident human right to liberty. Second addressed will be government spending brought in to address the economic depression which these lockdowns cause.

These arguments follow here.

Why Lockdowns Breach Any Consistent Model of Human Rights

Firstly, lockdowns are, by their nature, a violation of one's human rights. This will be a purely deontological argument on account of the concepts concerned. One MUST immediately take note of the modifier—*human.*

That is the most important indicator for the lay reader to understand; it means that these rights do not come from any government, party, state, document, god or any third party.

They exist and apply because you are human.

They are self-evident from and pertain to the nature of humanity itself.

They ought, then, to be universal? If only...

This, regrettably, marks the first point where the theory of human rights, or at least, the voluntarist theory, becomes distinct from the practice of human rights law. Ideas of inherent rights vested in some people (kings or other people previously thought to hold divine power) date back to time immemorial, but the entrenchment of the idea as something which could apply universally is most often dated to the Enlightenment.

The strongest efforts to apply it in practice have followed WWII and its horrors. This has come about both through nations committing to uphold and respect human rights between each other through treaties and creating their own regimens at home to protect whatever rights they agreed upon domestically.

The very summation above hints at the first two problems.

First, the vectoring of the rights.

Specifically, how this vectoring varies between what it should be and what it is. The theory of human rights would be derived deductively, at least on a normative level. One would determine which normative ethics (if stuck, read as: rules or procedures) are inherent to the operation and good living out of one's humanity. Whatever actions were needed pursuant to this would then be protected under rights.

This is not how the law has practically evolved. It has been imposed inductively by states, diplomats and bureaucrats. Each of these have their own distinct incentive to introduce permutations away from what might be deductively valid, and thereby, true, to any subject matter, human rights included. States especially have an obvious interest in curtailing rights which may be exercised adverse to their power.

Some readers may be thinking 'Not mine! My rulers would never do such a thing!' I challenge you; there is not one state which is completely guiltless—look hard enough, you'll find the evidence. The core of the first difference and the danger to one's thinking would then be this; the difference between how human rights should be thought of and how they have actually been thought of allows conflation between the two.

13

Readers may dismiss otherwise deductively valid arguments out of hand because their overlords and their so-called eminent domain demand that argument not apply. If you catch this thought or something to its effect flitting through your mind, I challenge you to recognise it as arbitrary, rebuke it accordingly, and continue reading.

The second practical problem at the outset is variance. It is a problem of provenance; relegating human rights to the doctrine of subsidiarity outside what is internationally agreed leads to further deviance from what is true and correct.

Different nations and different cultures have different histories and so their culture of rights have evolved differently. Yet all these constructs consist of units of humans, all of whom share unit equity in their humanity; all humans are created equal. Another contradiction then; if our humanity is not permuted and remains equal with our culture, nationality or whatever other characteristic, how on earth are rights self-evident from our humanity changed on those bases?

Again, the twin answers are obvious. First, they shouldn't be and second, they are not but merely dressed up as that for those who can either tolerate cognitive dissonance (AKA untruths) or do not care. The doctrine is changed on the basis of the first criticism; states have imposed their own versions of the doctrine, states are variant, their doctrines vary accordingly.

It is this, which introduces the inconsistency I so detest into something which should, by its nature, be consistent.

Subsidiarity is normally a good thing, it minimises informational corruption, increases accountability and generally makes people and entities more utility efficient.

However, this is not so where a matter of pure logical derivation applies.

As the great Yudkowsky might say, pure logic remains true in all universes and places and so by its nature (or in this case, all human universes) and so can never show you in which one, or where in a given one, you happen to live. Or rather here, it shouldn't. Your overlords would have you believe to the contrary for their own benefit.

Don't.

What then, is the voluntarist stance on human rights? What rights are there? Why are they there? Why are some which may be omitted from other doctrines not present?

Again, it would be both outside the remit of this book and a grave offence to tautologise the work of prior scholars in this field. For those wishing to explore more thoroughly, I suggest beginning with Rothbard's seminal *Man, Economy and State* available for free online and following your nose from there.

My brief summary would be this: humans own themselves. They either possess free will inherently, or by negative induction as any argument that they do not is self-defeating. It follows that they should be able to conduct all things within the scope of humanity's nature at will so long as they never infringe on that of another in the process.

You may have heard this idea contracted into the label of negative rights. Only these rights can exist in our view; there can be no right which violates another. Such a thing would be an aberration—illogical, self-contradictory and therefore, false on its own premises.

There can, therefore, be no positive rights (our first potentially controversial assertion), these being any imagined right which would require anyone else take any positive (hence the name) action (such as giving you their labour or a product thereof) to grant or maintain (as opposed to an omission, such as the right to life being manifested negatively in my omitting murder from my actions).

Three broad groups of rights exist within this domain of negative rights: first, those falling under life, second, those falling under liberty and third, those falling under property.

I will now briefly cover the first two areas; the third is covered in the argument against government intervention.

The Right to Life in Brief

You are alive! Congratulations! You may have noticed that, in the course of living, you have needed to follow certain procedures and have done so of your own volition. Not only that, but to live well, at least by your own means and reckoning, these procedures have shifted as you aged, grew and changed.

Consider the Maslovian Hierarchy.

For those unfamiliar, it is a model of evolving psychological needs, often referred to in developmental psychology. It starts with basic needs: 'food, water, warmth and rest'. From there it builds to safety, belonging, esteem and finally, self-actualisation.

The vast majority of readers may have had the first two tiers provided for them, yet they will understand through their pursuit of the last three. They may have also noticed the difficulty in compartmentalising and pursuing the upper criteria when the lower ones are out of place.

So the logic goes, no matter one's models and variations therein, that there are certain things which we all need to live well, and that there is definitely a structure to them, if not necessarily an outright linear progress.

It is also crucial to note that these things can be acquired without coercion.

Assuming competence, one can feed oneself, barter for security, aim to maximise one's sexual market value to secure a mate, so and so forth until the hierarchy is completely manifested. This even remains true where this assumption is not the case but remains a benevolent and caring figure in place to protect and support the individual in question.

Having established this, the question then likely follows to those outside the choir; why is the voluntarist objection to using a monopolist on violence to realise these positions universally so uncompromising?

The first element of reply would be that such phrasing is already generous; governments do not always intervene with the intention of bettering the lives of their subjects, especially outside the halcyon lands of the West.

The second element was already hinted at in some prior paragraphs. Simply because a government may be able to intervene in such a manner as to manipulate the positions of various people in life according to the furtherance of certain criteria.

It does not follow that there is a valid *a priori* argument, or any other argument for that matter, granting them the eminent domain to do so. Such an approach would necessarily involve the infringement of the capacities on some to live their lives to the full in the attempt of increasing some criterion. Just because there is unit equity between each other's lives, and each others right to life, it does not imply that a monopolist on the market for organised violence has any right to intervene so as to project that equity into the consequences resulting from one's decisions.

As before; decisions are the nature of life and equity does not mean equality.

Hence, we lay out the voluntarist position on the right to life in brief; like every other, it exists purely negatively and exists in just that way—protection of it is only to be invoked in threat or actual instance of violation, not some forward projection of its starting point.

The Right to Liberty in Brief

The right to liberty can be summated rather more briefly with the previous knowledge in hand. This is because it is derived from the prior right.

The right to liberty exists because it is necessary to the living of a good life. This was implied in the prior section and is also presumably implied through your own behaviour; you have presumably taken the initiative throughout your own life in living out what you want it to be.

In order to do this, you need the right to liberty and to act out your own desires so far as they do not infringe another's rights to do so. You may not be conscious of it unless you take time to actively reflect and appreciate it, or it manifests to you constantly by your own actions and use of it.

Granting this as a presupposition, one should then apply it to the specific context of the COVID-19 pandemic.

The right to life has not been questioned by any actor during this pandemic, at least those acting in good faith. Parties arguing for statist incursions who also happen to be well-intentioned in doing so (which may be a substantially smaller number than what first appears) argue for such incursions on the grounds of protecting this right. The right to liberty has been, chiefly on the grounds of its supposed imposition on the prior during times of pandemic.

Again, this nonargument which they mount is a sort of epistemic example of the *post hoc ergo propter hoc* fallacy. Just because the right to liberty is derived from the right to life, does not mean one can retroactively infringe on the right to liberty in the name of protecting the right to life.

The policies proposed may be sensible enough if they were to be practiced by individuals voluntarily; this is emphasised later in the chapter on Sweden and its approach to COVID-19.

Just because certain policies such as social distancing, shielding the vulnerable (though lockdowns seem more contestable on the evidence) may be sensible scientifically to stop a viral spread, it does inherently follow that any monopolist on the market for organised violence has a right to impose them under threat of that violence.

Those who catch COVID-19 and die are not the rule.

Deaths as a result of it are tragic, and should be minimised, of course. This is obvious, yet I am sure someone will attempt to attack this book on the grounds of not caring about those deaths and projecting virtue by comparison for my crime of questioning their statist idolatry.

Statists have done this before; they will do so again.

Men such as Piers Morgan felt the need to build the pulpit from which to preach their anti-Second Amendment cases out of the bones of massacred children due to the lack of a better argument, and then lecture down their perfumed noses at those they implied were morally inferior by nonarguments appealing to visceral emotion, rightfully felt but wrongfully placed.

Lockdown worshippers will doubtless hijack tragic COVID-deaths to defend their ego and virtue signalling investment in their nonargument. Charlatans and *agents provocateur* can use this strategy so effectively because our culture has elevated the perception of political correctness and emotional sensitivity to an end goal, to a god, rather than as the means it is.

God is no longer love, love is god.

We must strive to be different, to be honest, no matter whom we offend. Lives may depend on it, now, and in the future, if we surrender our liberties. Should we surrender them for one crisis now, we create an incentive for the manufacturing of further crises in which we will do the same.

As such, not an inch can be yielded.

Not. One. Step. Back.

I will not dishonestly advance the claims of survival rates being stratospheric, as some other civil libertarians have. This is because, even if antibody tests could be deployed amongst a significant percentage of the population to gauge a good result, whatever amount this represented would change during the experiment assuming a total amount infected less than 100%.

Far better to look at average rate of fatality per infection and then control for age; studies have so far produced variant results. Do not give in to advancing arguments which seem convenient for civil liberties but compromise the honesty of the position in the process.

The reason this is brought up is the burden of proof; it stands to reason if one is going to conceptualise rights consistently and honestly, if one is to accept any imposition at all there should be a much higher burden of proof in place than the simple chance that one's actions may endanger another's rights.

It is not enough proof for national house arrest to submit that the actions of a limited number subject to that action may endanger a certain number less than all. Consent defences, though again tempting, are only partial. It is difficult to sincerely mount an argument that everyone outside under the circumstances, knowingly or not, consents to the risk of infection. It would be harder still to argue, if not impossible, that those who meet those who happen to have been outside or have engaged in activity with a risk of infection (without having done so themselves; think your grandmother shielding in her bungalow), further consent to that same degree of risk by association.

If we mount an argument against social contract theory for presuming consent, we cannot presume it ourselves. As such, the defence of the right to liberty in this circumstance must remain on the grounds of its own inherent value.

The right to liberty may be derived from the right to life, but this does not mean that the right to liberty of all can be infringed, setting permanent precedent in an uncertain and ultimately temporary defence of the right to life.

Causal primacy does not imply total primacy.

The Voluntarist Stance against Economic Intervention in Brief

Beginning with the deontological aspect, we will assume two vectors for acquiring the money for the state to spend in its intervention; both can be shown to be illegitimate.

The first is taxation, which is morally equivalent to robbery (a forcible extraction of funds from you) unless one grants an exemption to it on behalf of some governmental righteousness. There is no valid *a priori* justification for this exemption, even in a democracy.

It is frustrating to see many 'conservatarian' commentators such as Ben Shapiro recognise this *prima facie* without engaging fully in the resulting realisation and shift in policy, which would be the intellectually honest thing to do. Shapiro himself encapsulates the idea in theory at least rather well: 'You voting to beat me up and take my money does not make it right for you to beat me up and take my money'.

This is because democratic voting normally justified by *jus sanguinis* is arbitrary to the first degree; you have no control over where you are born and cannot be said to have validly consented to any procedures enforced upon you by characteristics determined therefrom i.e. nationality and the logically illiterate 'social contract theory'.

Furthermore, there is no inherent *a priori* validity to a majority of people and anything they opine; most people can recognise this when pressed with *ad absurdum* examples but bring in convenient excuses (often based on emotion) when they like the policy being 'justified' on this basis. This works best where there is no *a priori* distinction between the two examples, just distinctions based on people's comfort with each of them, but still stands on an intellectual level regardless (e.g. proposing to someone an income tax rate at 40% and then 100%, both backed by the same majority at different points in time).

Hence, taxation, or any other appropriation of resources, to acquire this funding is an illegitimate exercise of violence against peaceful people who did not aggress the government exercising the violence in question and mere democracy is no defence.

The second vector is spending without taxation, either by directly printing the money, writing it off in debt or quantitative easing, or by some other monetary construct. This produces illegitimacies through two vectors; the first is that this debt must still be paid directly. Seeing as states claim eminent domain over their territories, the debt is passed onto all people who currently live and who may ever live in the territory so long as the state holds the debt to be live. This includes unborn children.

Whatever one may think of social contract theory and the capacity of those present at the time to consent to such spending, those only present in the future who will be liable for it definitely cannot be said to have consented.

For an easier picture, imagine if I walked into your child's school, or your own at the time when you were there if you do not have children. Imagine I then state that an arbitrary majority of a given arbitrary set of people had presumed to spend a given amount of money speculatively. We, after spending that money, were now foisting the corresponding liability in an unknown and undisclosed proportion (we do not know what figure they will pay and even if we did we won't tell them) to those children and any children they may later have.

Should they attempt to avoid this first liability when they grow up they may incur further liability of having more money deprived by fines through the same mechanism of a monopoly on violence enforcing the current liability, or failing that, be thrown and locked in a cage (jail and/or prison), again, pursuant to the same enforcement and derivation mechanisms.

Mechanisms which they, of course, being children and good, obedient, future wage slaves have no control over but are liable for in both its own costs of operation and whatever other costs it or its masters choose to impose upon them or some segment of them.

Take the resulting realisation. Abstract it to every nation that has ever been. You may feel some emotional relief for a moment on account of the conceptual distance from your own family. This is presumably before realising that this reflection of our current model is far worse because that means it's not just your children, childhood and lives; its <u>everyone's</u> children, childhoods and lives.

So what if we avoid repaying the sum entirely and ride off into the sunset of utopia never paying back the loans we grant ourselves? Isn't that a solution? Maduro thought so, but last time I checked that's not going so well for Venezuela. And it works psychologically right up until one remembers about inflation, which renders it both deontologically and consequentially unfit as an approach. An economic law so often misunderstood, it can be derived in its most basic form to be applied here from the idea that currency is a store of value.

This, combined with its other characteristics like ease of exchange is what renders it so valuable; precisely because it is a representative and store of value. If it were not this, it would be just another valueless trinket.

So, seeing as nations and/or economic blocs have engaged in the habit of neatly separating their own currencies from each other bar a few exceptions, the grand total amount of one currency may roughly be said to function as a store of the total value of its corresponding economy.

Economists will realise that this oversimplification falls apart as soon as one opens it up to interests such as those generated in FOREX markets or in comparative advantages between currencies based on their positions and relative values, against the trade balance of a given economy as well as currency pegging, but it stands for the purposes of the point about economies or key agents therein internally regulating spending, so I ask them to tolerate it for now.

If one was to, in this model, attempt to increase the real value of the goods and services in the economy, this would generate corresponding pressure on the currency. The spending, definitionally involving the generation of new monies within this model, is not equally distributed amongst agents in the economy but where the spending itself is directed.

This might seem a statement of the obvious but is important; it means that even where the value of the currency as a total normalises back to a representative of the total value of the economy in question to the same value before the spending, something which never happens practicably in the first place, the currency held before the spending by parties not involved with the spending in question is artificially and retroactively devalued. This is because their share of assets in the economy represented by the currency they hold comparatively shrinks against those who receive funds from the spending.

All this is done without asking those suffering devaluation and they cannot do anything about it without entering the market the spending concerns and chasing the artificial profit it brings.

Central banks and inflationary targets exacerbate this problem further.

Very often in the modern day the objective of central banks has been to bring inflation down but consider examples where they are mandated to aim for a certain level, normally around 2%. This is normally thought of as a way of both guaranteeing financial confidence in predictable inflation by year and a way of motivating people to work harder by forcing them to continually increase their value to at least match the background rate of inflation, or suffer a loss in welfare.

It is this second element which is so morally reprehensible.

Governments, central banks and bureaucrats, if not for their eminent domain, would likely have nothing to do with the bulk of transactions dominating your day-to-day life. Yet they insert their will through the currency you use; admittedly their officially minted currency, and one might argue implied consent to whatever the agenda of the agents of the mint is by using their products.

This consent would be at best implied and at worst outright uninformed in many cases across the population, though hopefully no longer yours for having read this book.

Consider the rightfully felt horror which would follow if we applied so low a standard of consent elsewhere, say sexual crimes. Similar implications on the moral level are present, just with different degrees of separation between the two contentious forces—that being the dubious or nonexistent nature of consent given and the violation of bodily autonomy.

With an arena like sexual crimes the violation of the first by the second is immediately and viscerally obvious, inspiring the strength of reaction it so rightfully does.

One could make a compelling argument for the same logic being present here, just through many more degrees of separation. You own your own labour. You own this because you own yourself and your labour is derived from you. You exchange it for goods and services, most probably money. This money, should you not immediately spend it and choose to stockpile some, as you almost certainly should, is artificially devalued by agents in charge of its regulation, who you almost certainly do not elect. These agents only have, as before, at best implied and at worst uninformed consent to do so even where one is so generous as to say it exists at all.

Hence, your labour has been artificially and retroactively devalued, along those lines and with similar moral implications; the ultimate being the violation of your bodily autonomy and self-ownership. It is this, which, no matter what you may think of some of his uglier writings (which are acknowledged as wrong and indefensible), as Dr. Ron Paul put it, ensures that there is not enough money for families year on year.

Hence, not only can inflation retroactively devalue goods and services exchanged in the past without consent, but also distorts current signals on the value of goods and services. Hence, one sees the illegitimacy of this method too.

Hayek's Local Knowledge Problem functions as a further consequential proof. The Local Knowledge problem states its revelation in its own name; people hold knowledge locally. Statistical aggregates cannot account for this, yet this is how central authorities plan decisions, at least when doing so rationally.

Even the best intentioned central authority quite simply cannot be as efficient an executive of the demands which a given piece of information creates as those whom it affects.

Hence, local action, local spending, local investment, corresponding to where the knowledge in question is held, produces the best results.

This has not been the case with the response to COVID-19 and is never the case with government spending.

Section 2—Sweden, Liberty's Last Bastion?

Worry often gives a small thing a big shadow.
An hour lost is often a year lost.
—Swedish Proverbs

WHATEVER GODS MAY or may not be, they must be thanked for the Swedes. COVID-19 was first confirmed to be present in Sweden on 31 January 2020; the first confirmed communal infection was on the 9 March around Stockholm, though travel-related clusters had broken out just prior to this point. The first tragic death came two days later.

Organisation

In order to fully understand the variance in the Swedish response to the crisis compared to many other nations, one must understand the peculiarities of the Swedish constitution[1] and how they applied

---

[1] *The Constitution of Sweden*, 2021

in this regard, especially where civil liberties are concerned.

The constitution contains a partial safeguard on freedom of movement for the people; this prevents a national lockdown (at least during peacetime). Some may be quick to immediately decry the example on this basis; that a nation which could never have locked down is no countering example to those which could.

I submit to the exact contrary—Sweden stands as one of the few examples of an alternative to glorified house arrest. The constitution also guards against ministerial rule, in contrast to a system like the UK.

Instead, localised knowledge of specialists and experts is invoked; the government is expected to defer on technical issues where possible. Here, this meant that the Public Health Agency (PHA) had just that, prime agency, to bring any actions regarding COVID-19 into effect in accordance with pre-existing law. This explains the central presence of the state epidemiologist, Anders Tegnell, in the country. Much discussion of the balance of democracy against technocracy rightly follows in any extrapolation of this model.

Many in my own UK have rightly criticised the Johnson government for resigning democratic responsibility to SAGE technocrats, I submit most probably in a dual-edged attempt to either claim proper humility in the event of success, and retain a scapegoat in the event of failure.

What seems to me to be the crucial difference is exactly what is formerly stated—where the UK promoted technocrats on the convenience of political circumstance and zeitgeist, the Swedish model specifically enshrines the scientists' position in policy direction.

The familiarity of the people with the presence of specialists in policy direction in turn affects the amount of political pressure which can be created by their direction.

Anders Tegnell was under fire regularly,[2] some would go as far as to say daily, during Sweden's management of the crisis.

Yet during this entire time his defenses were concise, pithy and matter of fact. The Swedish people are presumably used to the regular public accountability and scrutiny of scientists involved with the public domain just as they might any other politician.

On the other hand, I am relatively confident in asserting that most people in the UK would not be able to name the foremost doctors of SAGE, never mind their exact policies. One would, upon asking, likely be greeted with vague platitudes like '15 days to flatten the curve'[3] and, as we are now seeing on the Senate floor of the United States, language specifically designed to evade legal liability and prosecution,[4] rather than open discourse and accountability before the people these policies are supposedly meant to serve.

It is from this difference in culture that we see the difference in response to the elevated importance of public health officials and scientists in recent years.

In Sweden, it was simply an elevation of the usual manner of things. But in other polities which were and are not used to seeing scientists at the forefront of public policy, differing opinions emerged. Dr. Fauci in the U.S. swiftly became something of a

[2] https://www.ft.com/content/5cc92d45-fbdb-43b7-9c66-26501693a371

[3] Bendix, A. (2021). *Trump's 15-day plan to slow the coronavirus' spread is too short, experts say. Flattening the curve could take at least several more weeks.* Business Insider. Retrieved from:
https://www.businessinsider.com/coronavirus-white-house-15-day-plan-too-short-2020-3?op=1&r=US&IR=T

[4] Reynolds, G. (2021). *Officials like Fauci have undermined trust in government institutions.* The New York Post. Retrieved from https://nypost.com/2021/03/18/officials-like-fauci-have-undermined-trust-in-government-institutions/

national icon, to the point where, even if Rand Paul wanted to have him arrested for perjury on the Senate Floor, I doubt he could do so without taking on the appearance of Brutus.

The UK already pedestalises the NHS in a truly strange fashion; this facet of our discourse became even more pronounced in most left wing and supposedly 'centrist' and 'unbiased' publications. Meanwhile, the right's vigilance of selective reporting, such as the BBC broadcasting NHS workers who also happened to be either Labour party members or activists[5], became ever more hawkish.

It is illustrative of the general point that new models of management must be introduced slowly, but it will also be interesting to return to as and when the next crisis rolls around. If it is used again, how will people in nations which formerly never used such a policy react to its repetition; will it become just another Tuesday as in Sweden?

Or will the Anglosphere insist on separation of science and state, what little of it remains that is?

This approach also relies on discipline to function, true enough. Swedes are expected to follow 'non-voluntary guidance' issued by the relevant government bodies and have done so with far greater degrees of stringency compared to other nations. At least, I find it worth noting, the Swedish government is half honest by calling the guidance 'non-voluntary', where other governments have attempted to obfuscate the language surrounding what are truthfully orders enforced by government backed violence entirely.

'NHS guidance' and 'CDC guidance' being two such examples.

This has resulted in freedom of assembly being limited in

[5] Singh, A. (2021). BBC defends Panorama show that used Labour activists to criticise lack of PPE. *The Telegraph*. Retrieved from https://www.telegraph.co.uk/news/2020/04/29/bbc-defends-panorama-show-used-labour-activists-criticise-lack/

Sweden, as far as the constitutional framework allows, through laws enacted pursuant to agency recommendations, such as bans on gatherings of more than 50 and visits to nursing homes. Secondary schools and universities have been completely closed but primary schools have been kept open, in part on the rationale of keeping care workers separate from young children as much as possible.

Further direct recommendations from agencies to government focused on extending welfare to those whose living would be affected and reducing vectors for infection throughout the population.

After establishing the summary; it would be tempting to immediately jump into argumentation showing why this approach is better in all possible terms compared to others in the current times.

However, that would omit an arguably critical element in place up to 15 years beforehand. That is to say, the first national pandemic response plan was drafted for Sweden in 2005 in response to the avian flu outbreak in the same year. An important revision came in 2008 with the formation of a specifically empowered and defined National Pandemic Group.[6]

The full version in Swedish is available to read here for those sufficiently knowledgeable.[7]

Under this plan, the PHA of Sweden is given broad responsibility for tracking diseases with the potential to develop

---

[6] Public Health Agency. (2019, December 19). Pandemiberedskap. Hur vi förbereder oss—ett kunskapsunderlag—Folkhälsomyndigheten. Retrieved October 14, 2020, from:
https://www.folkhalsomyndigheten.se/publicerat-material/publikationsarkiv/p/pandemiberedskap-hur-vi-forbereder-oss-ett-kunskapsunderlag/
[7] Tegnell, A. (2009, May). Nationell plan för pandemisk influensa. Retrieved October 14, 2020, from:
https://sverigesradio.se/diverse/appdata/isidor/files/406/6991.pdf

into pandemics and further, if necessary, convene the wider Group. This Group in turn complements the Agency with further sub-agencies: the Civil Contingencies Agency, Medical Products Agency, National Board of Health and Welfare and the Work Environment Authority.

Further, also present are representatives from each county's administrative board and the Association of Local Authorities and Regions (an employer's agency). While this may all seem terribly technocratic or bureaucratic (and the author would to some extent be inclined to agree), consider the alternative within the statist context; bumbling ministerial rule which has had legions of unintended consequences and infringed liberties uncounted.

In an attitude which the rest of the world would do well to learn from, the Swedes also have a notably self-sufficient and subsidiary approach to responsibility (perhaps gleaned from centuries of collectively felt geographical realities and corresponding historical experience.)

In short, by the Swedes reckoning, if you're responsible for something during normalcy, when crisis comes, you remain responsible—this help explain the discipline of the Swedish populace in following 'guidance' compared to other countries. This stands in stark contrast to the rest of the world where citizens seem to have in large part resigned any individual responsibility upwards to the collective 'responsibility' of their rulers; Swedish PM Stefan Löfvén exhorted the populace to take personal responsibility.[8]

Further, I submit that the Swedish response should, once and for all, prove the epistemic fallacies at play here in most statist

---

[8] Stenberg, E. (2020, March 27). Ewa Stenberg: Löfven vill hellre övertyga än förbjuda. Retrieved October 16, 2020, from: https://www.dn.se/nyheter/sverige/ewa-stenberg-lofven-vill-hellre-overtyga-an-forbjuda/

modelling and thinking more generally. I not deny the existence of opposing incentives for individuals in question as opposed to the rest of the nation at large; someone infected with COVID-19 may still derive a large amount of utility from engaging in outdoor activities and socialising despite the potentially massive social cost from these actions for example. It is perfectly possible to think of many other examples which would be variations on this theme.

It is in the same breath true that the social interest in question, if it can accurately be labelled 'social' at all without unfairly presuming the existence of such a thing as a body worthy of separate moral consideration from each individual, is little more than the agglomeration of other individual incentives set apart from one specific instance and then weighted accordingly.

Treating that 'social' interest or incentive as something magically different on account of that agglomeration and one's inability to dissect and label every point of significance and divergence therein, perhaps combined with some warm fuzzy feeling one may associate with the concept (others anecdotally report it, yet it remains foreign to me!), is bound to lead to the inconsistent conclusions and subsequently (and also ironically) social dissatisfaction observed today as a consequence of that inconsistency.

This, I submit, emerges precisely because those who predicate their models on the existence of society as having some differentiating 'x factor' from a collection of individuals are inserting a fudge factor into their modelling to pre-empt precisely the above objection; that nobody, them included, can accurately model every point of significance within that agglomeration. So better to inject their own best estimate and cross their fingers?

If the Swedish counter-example doesn't prove the invalidity of such a reaction and way of thinking clear for all time, it is unclear what will.

Preparation

Having established what agencies are in place to handle the question, we can now move to examine their preparedness in this case.

The first, notable difference here to other portions of the world is the first operational presumption; the Swedes assumed that another pandemic would affect them,[9] even in their frigid and removed geography, within 50 years at most.[10]

In terms of the system's capability for the detection of a new biological threat, maintaining a low risk environment and reporting to everyone else. Concerns were raised, to be manifested later, about how well the system could handle the stress such a pandemic would impose on the national healthcare fabric. This was chiefly based on two factors: hospital beds per capita[11] and ICU beds per capita,[12] both of which were below the EU average in Sweden's case.

Another Swedish peculiarity must be noted here; their previously supreme system of military medicine had atrophied

---

[9] Winehav, M., Lindstedt, U., Kallstrom, D., & Borg, K. (2013). Risker och förmågor 2013. Retrieved October 15, 2020, from https://rib.msb.se/filer/pdf/27331.pdf

[10] Bratt, A. (2014, September 28). Så är Sveriges skydd mot en pandemi. Retrieved October 15, 2020, from http://www.dn.se/nyheter/vetenskap/sa-ar-sveriges-skydd-mot-en-pandemi

[11] OECD. (n.d.). Health Care Resources. Retrieved October 15, 2020, from: http://stats.oecd.org/index.aspx?DataSetCode=HEALTH_REAC

[12] Rhodes, A., Ferdinande, P., Flaatten, H., Guidet, B., Metnitz, P., & Moreno, R. (2012, October 1). "The variability of critical care bed numbers in Europe". Retrieved October 15, 2020, from https://doi.org/10.1007%2Fs00134-012-2627-8

away almost entirely since 1990.

30 years previously the system stood at 50 hospitals treating 10,000 patients and performing 1,000 surgeries a day plus additional equipment to handle 150,000 casualties, though its unknown exactly how well the last element would factor into a viral pandemic of this kind. By 2020, there were only 2 medical units left with 80 standard and a further 16 ICU beds with no procedure for storing preparing medical equipment ahead of time.

It is worth noting that some argue privatisations, which voluntarists normally praise, could be argued to crop up in a negative light here—the Swedish drug supply was privatised in 2009.[13]

The most common argument running thereafter is that a lack of regulation gave no incentive to private entities to maintain a large stock of medicines, thereby leading to failure when the pandemic hit. Private entities have little incentive to spend money planning for unlikely scenarios; one should not anchor on the consequences the Coronavirus has had and retroactively project those consequences as an interpretation that it should have been easily predictable—part of the very reason it has had the consequences in question is precisely because its emergence was not foreseen.

If one needs further confirmation of this, look at how shocking the emergence of COVID-19 was in arenas with similarly mixed or entirely publicly held health regimes. Did they anticipate it coming years in advance?

No?

Then no systemic point is proven.

---

[13] Runblom, K. (2009, January 15). S, MP och V vill riva upp apoteksbeslut. Retrieved October 16, 2020, from https://sverigesradio.se/sida/artikel.aspx?programid=83&artikel=256 9863

Compounding this issue in Sweden is the fact that, whilst privatisation only occurred in 2009, reductions in the parallel military medical capacity began in the 90's. There is no way, from the context, to know if the private firms or government attention being directed elsewhere is at fault to a greater degree in this case with events manifesting together in this instance being so far distanced in time. Further, it will be demonstrated in the conclusion that, on the whole, privatised systems of healthcare have handled the pandemic better than those held in public trust.

Comparative advantage is also 'criticised' here by some; the economic law had caused the Swedish healthcare system to depend entirely on imported medicine with no home-grown manufacturing ability, due to high operating costs in the country. This had been identified as a potential point of failure as early as 2013 if those supply lines were to be cut in the event of a crisis and repeated until 2019 without action.[14]

That criticism doesn't make autarky the right action to take automatically and analysis of main points of failure in the Swedish approach doesn't point to supply of medicine as a key issue; it's worth noting that on that basis perhaps attention was focused in the wrong places by those seeking to mitigate events.

Response

The response of the Swedish government was precisely parameterised from the outset; limit infections to within the capacity of the national healthcare system. As a secondary objective, aim to ensure local regions have necessary resources to better make use of subsidiary organs in the healthcare system[15].

---

[14] Leth, E. (2019). Resursförstärkt läkemedelsförsörjning inför kris, höjd beredskap och krig: Kunskapsunderlag. Lund, Sweden: Lunds universitet.

[15] Government Offices of Sweden. (2018, August 7). Crisis

Major advisory actions first came from the PHA first came on the 10th of March pursuant to indications of domestic community infections rather than those carrying into the country. Those with any kind of respiratory infection were advised to cease socialising and working where there was a risk of a spread.

6 days later, it was recommended that those older than 70 should limit close contact with others—by the end of the month a survey showed 93% of those concerned were following the directions,[16] along with a further recommendation that all in the workforce work from home where possible.[17]

Surveys a month later were reported to show that roughly 50% of the population had managed to follow this.[18]

With infections continuing apace, the next day all secondary schools and universities were instructed to use 'distanced learning'; these regulations held until 15 June.

It is at this point that we should also examine the consequential benefits felt by Sweden pursuant to its approach.

The figure below extracted from a BBC article on the subject,

management in the Government Offices. Retrieved October 16, 2020, from:
https://www.government.se/government-policy/emergency-preparedness/crisis-management-in-the-government-offices/
[16] Novus. (2020, April 06). Coronastatus 0331. Retrieved October 16, 2020, from https://novus.se/coronastatus-0331/
[17] Personer över 70 bör begränsa sociala kontakter tills vidare - Folkhälsomyndigheten. (2020, March 16). Retrieved October 16, 2020, from https://www.folkhalsomyndigheten.se/nyheter-och-press/nyhetsarkiv/2020/mars/personer-over-70-bor-begransa-sociala-kontakter-tills-vidare/
[18] Henley, J. (2020, April 15). Critics question Swedish approach as coronavirus death toll reaches 1,000. Retrieved October 16, 2020, from https://www.theguardian.com/world/2020/apr/15/sweden-coronavirus-death-toll-reaches-1000

in turn citing Eurostat, encapsulates the point quite handily.[19] As it
shows, the Swedish performance was above average for the EU and
blows other major economies which far exceed its absolute size out
of the water. Yet already objections will clang from rooftops
lamenting the inadequacy of GDP as an indicator for specific
economic analyses.

Sweden's economy is doing better than other European nations
% change in quarterly GDP

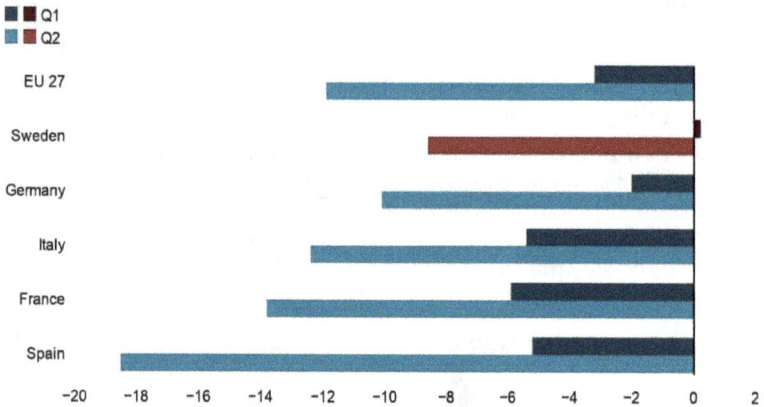

Source: Eurostat/Statistics Sweden (Q2 fig)   BBC

These are *prima facie* accepted on their own terms but it must be
remembered that a broad strokes comparison suffices for the
immediate term, especially when combined for the fact that it will
be difficult to isolate the different approaches and their effects
elsewhere, though unemployment and inflation are becoming
clearer, chiefly as a result of the Biden administration across the

[19] Savage, M., 2021. *Coronavirus: Sweden's economy hit less hard by
pandemic.* [online] BBC News. Available at:
https://www.bbc.co.uk/news/business-53664354 [Accessed 19 May
2021].

pond.

More classic goalpost shifting will follow from authoritarian elements who even now want to keep your rights from ever returning to you.

It will suddenly not be enough that Sweden avoided economic catastrophe; everyone older than a toddler will remember the initial claim that there would be scant difference to the economy as a result of the Swedish policy, just excess death.[20]

Now it's suddenly all important that Sweden not suffer even one more death than its neighbours, for surely, any result to the contrary is a condemnatory failure, or if at least, our good friends at the Guardian are once again to be believed...[21]

For any curious as to the results of deaths in Sweden, this graph[20] serves as another encapsulation from March of 2020 though July and just into August:

[20] Miltimore, J., 2021. *Sweden's Actual COVID-19 Results Compared to What Modelers Predicted in April | Jon Miltimore.* [online] Fee.org. Available at: <https://fee.org/articles/sweden-s-actual-covid-19-results-compared-to-what-modelers-predicted-in-april/> [Accessed 19 May 2021].

[21] Geoghegan, P., 2021. *Now the Swedish model has failed, it's time to ask who was pushing it | Peter Geoghegan.* [online] The Guardian. Available at:
<https://www.theguardian.com/commentisfree/2021/jan/03/swedish-model-failed-covid-19> [Accessed 19 May 2021].

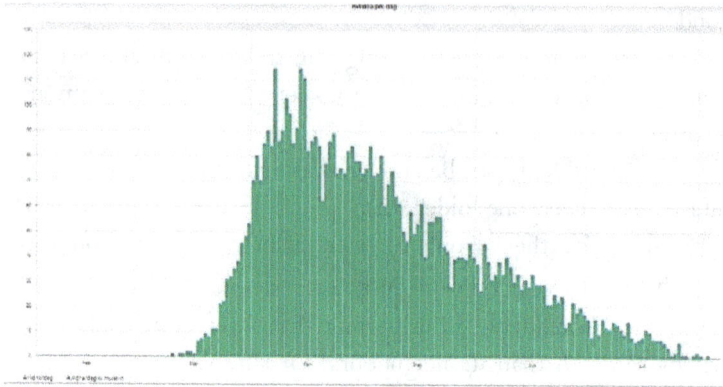

This in turn yields a number of outputs as the FEE puts it: 5,763 deaths (1/1775 people in the total population), 67% of deaths over 80 years old, 90% of deaths over 70 years old, 99% of deaths with pre-existing conditions, No deaths under 20 and 60 deaths under 50 years of age (for some 1/120,000 of the in-range pop.) Though the data will still be evolving throughout the remainder of 2021, this data hardly seems condemning of the Swedish approach, especially when compared to their ranking by Johns Hopkins.

Coverage

The Swedish approach was far from perfect from any point of view.

This shows up most clearly in their ban on gatherings. The 11th of March, which also marked the first death, brought in bans on gatherings larger than 500, under threats of fines and imprisonment, until further notice.[22]

It was at this point then that we can say that any semblance of

---

[22] Filip Persson, S. (2020, March 11). Klart: Inga evenemang med fler än 500 besökare. Retrieved October 16, 2020, from https://www.gp.se/nyheter/sverige/klart-inga-evenemang-med-fler-%C3%A4n-500-bes%C3%B6kare-1.25224161

voluntarism went out of the window in the Swedish approach, though it likely wasn't considered to being with. This was enhanced to cover gatherings larger than 50 on the 27th of March.[23] The expansion on the 27th also expanded the areas of the ban's application to entertainment and markets. Press conferences were held every day at 2 PM local time for citizens with representatives from the government agencies responsible for managing the pandemic within the country.

This is not likely the area of interest for readers of this book however; more likely international coverage which picked up precipitously after the virus began to spread in the country.

It is particularly worth emphasising that, at this stage, it appears that the only key deontological difference between the Swedish approach and those taken elsewhere is the eschewing of a total lockdown per the constitutional safeguards; other 'guidance' was still enforced by threat of government violence should the individuals concerned not comply. 'Guidance' indeed...

There may be consequential differences in the degrees of social distancing enforced across nations, at least explicitly, but, as before, the open admission that the guidance was 'non-voluntary', means that the deontological alignment is the same, all else is semantics and spin.

Despite the overwhelming similarities, media portrayal outside of the country ran to the contrary. Six descriptors were chiefly used to describe the approach at its outset: 'lax', 'laissez-faire', 'unorthodox', 'radical', 'extreme' or even 'Russian Roulette.' Some outlets maintained pretensions of neutral coverage, others

---

[23] Förbud mot allmänna sammankomster med fler än 50 personer. (2020, March 27). Retrieved October 16, 2020, from https://www.krisinformation.se/nyheter/2020/mars/ytterligare-begransning-sammankomster

did no such thing (see The Guardian).[24]

This changed across time; accusations of prioritising economic stability over lives (a falsely dichotomous argument in the first place) became speculation that the 'Swedish method' might be more 'durable' or 'sustainable' in the long run.[25]

Then the 'herd immunity' descriptions followed—the worst of this was perpetuated by President Trump who used the 'great suffering' in Sweden as a consequence of the 'herd immunity' strawman there in order to justify his stricter social distancing measures.[26]

Foreign minister Ann Linde insisted that there was no substantially different 'so-called Swedish strategy'; the Swedish goal was the same as everyone else: save lives, slow the spread and increase manageability for the health system.[27] Lena Hallengren, the Minister for Health and Social Affairs, elaborated further, reporting only two major differences between Sweden's approach and the rest of the world: keeping schools open and not enforcing a

---

[24] Robertson, D. (2020, March 30). *They are leading us to catastrophe: Sweden's coronavirus stoicism begins to jar.* The Guardian. Retrieved October 17, 2020, from:
https://www.theguardian.com/world/2020/mar/30/catastrophe-sweden-coronavirus-stoicism-lockdown-europe

[25] Svenska Institutet. (2020, April 22). *Samtalet om Sverige* [Scholarly project]. In *Svenska Institutet.* Retrieved October 17, 2020, from https://si.se/app/uploads/2020/04/samtalet-om-sverige-2020-04-22.pdf

[26] Sweden says Trump criticism of coronavirus strategy 'factually wrong'. (2020, April 8). *The Straits Times.* Retrieved October 17, 2020, from https://www.straitstimes.com/world/europe/sweden-says-trump-criticism-of-coronavirus-strategy-factually-wrong

[27] Clason, S. (2020, April 9). Ann Linde: "Finns många myter om svenska strategin". *Expressen.* Retrieved October 17, 2020, from https://www.expressen.se/nyheter/ann-linde-finns-manga-myter-om-svenska-strategin/

'lockdown'[28], or, to remove the euphemism, national house arrest sans *habeus corpus*.

One of the most persistent critics of this method was immunologist Cecilia Söderberg-Nauclér[29], who was later quoted in the Guardian, but overall academic response, at least within the country, has been at least neutral, if not positive.[30]

All of the Swedish defences of their response remains true of course. Then-President Trump lying and misappropriating circumstances elsewhere to justify his own policies in classic authoritarian fashion is nothing new. And the Republicans wonder why they have issues marketing themselves to consistent libertarians...It remains true that the Swedish aim was still to save lives, which they seem to have achieved just as well as most other nations, if not better. If that approach also preserves liberty, so much the better.

Parties in the Riksdag, the Swedish national assembly, were also hesitant to invoke debate over the response, in a display of unity again standing in contrast to other politicians around the world. All parties bar one out of the Riksdag declared a *borgfred* or 'truce' (far more honest political language than the sanitised

---

[28] Sweden isn't on a national lockdown amid coronavirus—Here's why. (2020, April 22). Retrieved October 17, 2020, from https://www.cnbc.com/video/2020/04/22/sweden-isnt-on-a-national-lockdown-amid-coronavirus-heres-why.html

[29] Samtalet om Sverige. (2020, April 4). *Samtalet om Sverige* [Scholarly project]. In *Svenska Institutet*. Retrieved October 17, 2020, from https://si.se/app/uploads/2020/04/samtalet-om-sverige-2020-04-15.pdf

[30] Sundholm, M. (2020, March 20). Kommentar: Sverige har valt en egen linje i coronakrisen och håller fast vid den. *Svenska Yle.* Retrieved October 17, 2020, from: https://svenska.yle.fi/artikel/2020/03/20/kommentar-sverige-har-valt-en-egen-linje-i-coronakrisen-och-haller-fast-vid-den

euphemisms found elsewhere).[31]

The only party out of the Riksdag, the Sweden Democrats, disagreed and called for school closures,[32] whilst the Moderate Party, the chief opposition in the Riksdag said through leader Ulf Kristersson that eventual evaluation will be needed, 'but not now.'

This didn't last long. Criticism came for Löfvén in May on a supposedly low number of tests; in contrast to promises to raise tests to 100,000 a week. Researchers started earlier, launching an attack on Tegnell on the 14th of April. An article penned by 22 scientists claimed that 'chaos in the healthcare system' [33] and that there 'was no transparency regarding the data used in agency models'—this despite the fact that all data is available on the PHA website through a spreadsheet.[34]

There are difficulties in comparing death rates objectively given differing methodologies, a point Tegnell himself made well[35].

---

[31] Holmqvist, A. (2020, June 3). Regeringen styr riket, jag leder regeringen, vi fattar besluten. *Aftonbladet.* Retrieved October 17, 2020, from:
https://www.aftonbladet.se/nyheter/samhalle/a/LAwVRx/regeringen-styr-riket-jag-leder-regeringen-vi-fattar-besluten

[32] Lönegård, C. (2020, March 19). Åkesson vill stänga skolorna – omedelbart. *Svenska Dagbladet.* Retrieved October 17, 2020, from https://www.svd.se/jimmie-akesson-vill-stanga-skolorna—omedelbart

[33] Folkhälsomyndigheten har misslyckats - nu måste politikerna gripa in. (2020, April 24). *Dagens Nyheter.* Retrieved October 17, 2020, from https://www.dn.se/debatt/folkhalsomyndigheten-har-misslyckats-nu-maste-politikerna-gripa-in/

[34] Saleem, N. (Writer). (2020, April 14). *Forskare om Sveriges strategi: "Kommer att bli kaos"* [Television broadcast]. Sweden. Retrieved October 17, 2020, from:
https://sverigesradio.se/sida/artikel.aspx?programid=83&artikel=7451820

[35] Lann, R., & Häkkinen, L. (2020, April 14). Tegnell's response to the sharp criticism in DN debate: Fundamental inaccuracies. *SVT Nyheter.*

Italy and others, he stated, only counted deaths in hospitals and as such had a more conservative estimate of the likely death toll compared to Sweden, which could explain how Sweden was seeming to close to those countries if one was to compare the data each nation was putting out without acknowledging the methodological differences.

Tegnell also did invaluable work in questioning the scientific basis of lockdowns; if not for him I fear the question may never have been seriously asked elsewhere at all.[36]

Whilst the prior mentioned civic responsibility helped mitigate the need for one in Sweden, it still does to criticise the 'science' of lockdowns in their own right. With all the facts laid out, we can begin the process of moving to debate the merits of the policies through varying vectors, both deontological and consequential.

In order to make that ascertainment, a comparative vector must be found.

We begin with the remainder of the EU.

Conclusions on Sweden

So what is to be gained from the Swedish approach?

At the most obvious level there are many lessons. The value of ironclad constitutional guarantees on liberties, requiring supermajorities to overturn has, once again, been proven. On the level of mindset, personal accountability to oneself and those around you (my atomistic tendencies forbid me from going so far

Retrieved October 17, 2020, from orskare-kritiska-til-fhm-lat-politikerna-ta-over

[36] Paterlini, M. (2020, April 21). 'Closing borders is ridiculous': The epidemiologist behind Sweden's controversial coronavirus strategy. *Nature*. Retrieved October 18, 2020, from: https://www.nature.com/articles/d41586-020-01098-x

as invoking community), modern 'woke' Westerners, often desperate to find any excuse to disregard personal responsibility, may look more thoroughly to the Nordic 'socialist utopias' they so often point to.

I won't entertain that non-argument any further; Dinesh D'Souza already reduced it to bedrock, but the lesson remains.

Statisticians and others may argue that we lack a sufficient number of anti-lockdown polities to run any kind of macrological comparison against those which locked down gladly. That is to say, there aren't enough Swedens to compare against the Chinas and UKs to fairly say that the Swedish outcome of a largely successful management combined with a lack of lockdown is best explained by policy, anomaly, or anything inbetween.

Let us, *prima facie* grant this, though if you find a way to refute it, do so with all guns blazing. If you can't, don't panic. Every deontological argument we make here, before and after holds firm, utterly unaffected. As long as you hold those important, any consequential mitigation is of minimal effect.

Furthermore, if I may pre-empt those who will may advance this half-argument with the other half which some will no doubt conveniently leave unsaid, I will. Namely, that there is only one way to complete the experiment that half-argument is nominally based on. That is to adopt the Swedish approach and mindset more widely when the next pandemic comes.

By the same logic which would deny the overwhelming proof of Sweden against lockdown worshippers, it cannot be overwhelmingly defeated, by lack of both a poor outcome and a large enough class of similar approaches to make an overall doctrinal analysis.

So, it follows that if both sides were to take the fair and impartial scientific spirit, they would seek to, at least notionally and further assuming no presumption of difference between the two approaches on counts of objection, spread the model in minority so as to balance out the sample sizes of nations come next time. That way, we can run the experiment fairly and come to a genuine conclusion.

Suggest this, and I anticipate you will either be met with accusations of callousness or absurdity, perhaps both. The intention of the half-argument is revealed—it was merely lockdown worshippers appropriating statistics and science for their own end; promptly throwing it aside as soon as following the demands of the scientific method resulted in anything they didn't like.

Some of you may accept the Swedish approach as all the consequential defeat of lockdowns you need. If so, liberty has prevailed in this instance and we may grant ourselves a moment's reprieve and celebration.

Some of you may not.

If you find yourself thinking this way, I challenge you to first of all rebuke the deontological argument made at the start. If you cannot, then your objection may simply be referred to capricious Lady time—more diseases will come and the objection will, assuming liberty remains in some corner of the earth, either be borne out or not. If you think you can, what relevance were the consequential arguments in the first place?

Either way, the only honest solution is to run the models against each other under fairer scenarios or walk away content with your own openly authoritarian worldview.

As before, we must thank whatever powers that be for the Swedish defence of liberty, and, far more importantly, carry it forwards from here.

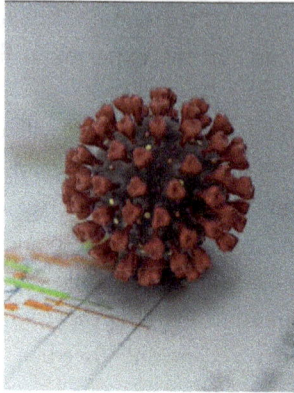

Section 3—A Plague 700 Years on, COVID-19 in Europe

If one rejects laissez-faire on account of man's fallibility and moral weakness, one must also for the same reason reject any every kind of government action.

—Ludwig von Mises

THE WORLD HEALTH ORGANISATION (WHO) first began to consider Europe the active centre of the COVID-19 pandemic on the 13th of March 2020. This was justified on the grounds that the number of new daily cases became greater than those in China came on this day.[37]

---

[37] Fredericks, B. (2020, March 13). WHO says Europe is new epicenter of coronavirus pandemic. New York Post. Retrieved October 18, 2020, from:
https://nypost.com/2020/03/13/who-says-europe-is-new-epicenter-of-coronavirus-pandemic/

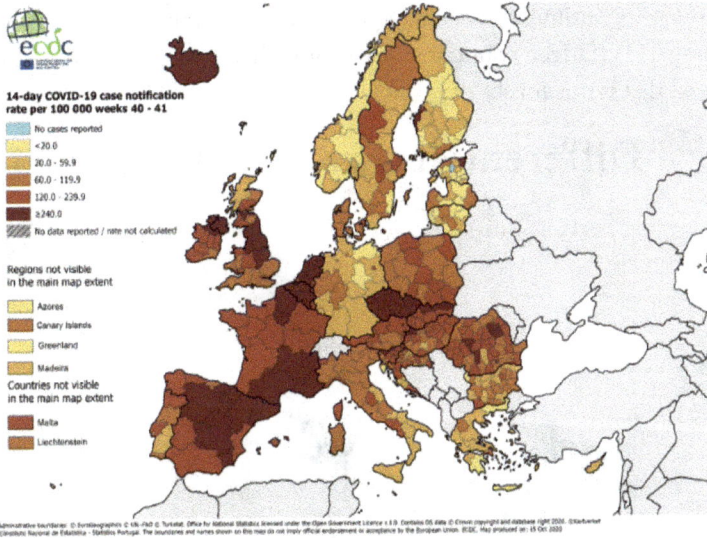

Figure 1
A graphical display by colour overlaying a map of Europe showing the notification of COVID cases every 2 weeks per 100,000 people 40-41 weeks from the first detected time the virus entered Europe. Accurate 18 October 2020.[38]

By the 17th of March, all countries within Europe had reported at least one case, with Montenegro being the last to do so. As of the time of writing all countries in Europe bar the Vatican have recorded at least one death from COVID-19, though, as before, methodologies vary. Cases then doubled across most countries every 3-4 days, though some reported doubling as swift as every 48

---

[38] EU, ECDC. (2020, October 18). COVID-19 Situation Update for the EU/EEA and the UK, as of 18 October 2020. Retrieved October 18, 2020, from:
https://www.ecdc.europa.eu/en/cases-2019-ncov-eueea

hours.[39] Continuing its bucking of trends, Montenegro became the first COVID-free country in the world though it only managed to hold this status for 44 days.

Differentiators and Indicators

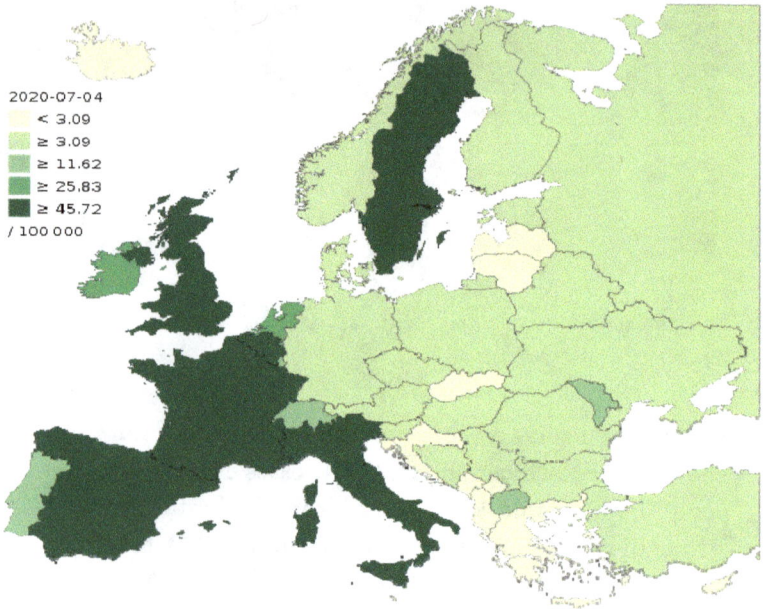

Figure 2
Cumulative number of deaths per 100,000 inhabitants
from COVID-19 in Europe.[40]

[39] Ritchie, H., Oritz-Ospina, E., Beltekian, D., Mathieu, E., Hasell, J., MacDonald, B.,...Roser, M. (2020, October 18). *Coronavirus Pandemic (COVID-19)*. Retrieved October 18, 2020, from Our World In Data.

[40] Commons, W. (2020, March 30). Cumulative number of deaths per 100,000 inhabitants from COVID-19 in Europe. [Digital image]. Retrieved October 19, 2020, from:
https://upload.wikimedia.org/wikipedia/commons/6/68/Persons_di

The graph above provides our first chief indicator.

Readers will notice that the relatively anti-lockdown Sweden is at the same tier as the UK, France, Spain, Belgium and Italy in terms of cumulative death. Large European states (read as, remove Belgium, insert Germany) also made statisticians and analysts lives much easier by all responding, at least as far as large governmental actions were concerned, all within the same month of March, at least in the first iteration of action before any 'second wave' is taken into account.

See the shading coded Figure 3 (below) for precise dates:

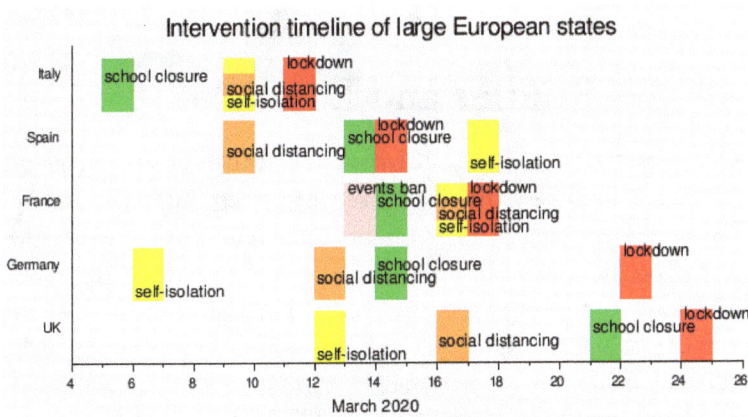

Figure 3

A timeline of interventions to prevent the spread of COVID-19 across the month of March by Italy, Spain, France, Germany and the UK.[41]

Performing a simple inductive analysis without diving too far down

---

ed_due_to_coronavirus_COVID-19_per_capita_in_Europe.svg

[41] Commons, W. (2020, March 26). Intervention Timeline of Large European States [Digital image]. Retrieved October 19, 2020, from https://upload.wikimedia.org/wikipedia/en/timeline/38a84a715770f a38483d79abdffa28e2.png

the rabbit hole of statistics, comparing the samples from the two figures, we can see that Germany is the anomaly of those sampled in Figure 3 in terms of cumulative deaths per Figure 2.

So the immediate question would be, why did Germany fair so much better than the other four states in Figure 3 given its longer spread of interventions across the month, especially compared to Italy? Surely, you would expect the nations which were the quickest to transition to total lockdown would come out the best as transmission vectors would be minimised; no matter how long it took symptoms to manifest in each person?

This is a question those arguing for lockdowns and further government intervention have yet to answer for…

Studies and Discussion

Of course, to cease the analysis there would be disingenuous. There are multiple criteria against which these interventions can be considered, such as infection rate, infections across the breadth of a population, mortality rates and recovery rates amongst others. Thankfully, a brilliant study featured in The Lancet did a lot of the work for advocates on all sides by compiling a large amount of the facts for them. The study tested for various correlations associated with government responses, available here.[42] To quote the findings in abstract removing the mathematical apparatus for ease of understanding:

> *Increasing COVID-19 caseloads were associated*
> *with countries with higher median population age*

---

[42] Chaudhry, R., Dranitsaris, G., Mubashir, T., Bartoszko, J., & Riazi, S. (2020). A country level analysis measuring the impact of government actions, country preparedness and socioeconomic factors on COVID-19 mortality and related health outcomes. *EClinicalMedicine, 25*, 100464. doi:10.1016/j.eclinm.2020.100464

and longer time to border closures from the first reported case. Increased mortality per million was significantly associated with higher obesity prevalence and per capita gross domestic product. Reduced income dispersion reduced mortality and the number of critical cases. Rapid border closures, full lockdowns, and wide-spread testing were not associated with COVID-19 mortality per million people. However, full lockdowns and reduced country vulnerability to biological threats (i.e. high scores on the global health security scale for risk environment) were significantly associated with increased patient recovery rates.

And the broader interpretation:

In this exploratory analysis, low levels of national preparedness, scale of testing and population characteristics were associated with increased national case load and overall mortality.

Let's break down each of these statements from the study in short order and from there move to examine the worth of government action:

1. An older median population correlated with a higher COVID caseload.

If you were to say to someone that older people suffered worse with viral infections in general, you'd be stating the obvious; the fact is well-documented if not as well understood.

The question then follows as to how COVID-19 itself behaves within this frame.

One PMC study divides it along the lines of the 65 year mark; aggregating for those 65 and over against all those under shows that those over 65 represent 80% of all hospitalisations and die 23 times more often than the younger aggregate as a result of the virus.[43]

Other commentators have used logarithmic scales of severity, saying that: 'COVID gets about 10 times worse for every 20 years you age.' Meaning here that if we were to give a hypothetical unit of 1 'COVID-Severity' as an aggregate of the total welfare loss endured to those aged 0-20, it would be 10 units for those aged 21-40, 100 units for those aged 41-60 and so on.

Surely then it follows, any rational government intervention should be stratified on that basis across the population, rather than acting in broad strokes?

This is perfectly conceivable without assigning an artificial value to life, obviously a sacrosanct value. One could fairly easily imagine a system of utility calculus where one takes the cost of each intervention expressed in whatever currency is relevant, compare it against the projected harm of not taking that action and, even assuming that calculus comes down in favour of intervention (as Sweden proves, not necessarily a given), modulate the action to be taken against the severity each age group would encounter.

This is still possible as a workable methodology even if one is so statist as to disregard the possibility of a more individually disciplined approach at all, or holds life so sacrosanct that even any economic calculus which may invoke it to the second degree cannot even be considered, no matter the consequential outcome of that comfortably enforced and faux-deontologically justified

---

[43] Mueller, A. L., McNamara, M. S., & Sinclair, D. A. (n.d.). *Why does COVID-19 disproportionately affect older people? PMC.* doi:10.18632/aging.103344

ignorance.

Even if (and, the author despairs, doubtlessly where) one works on the basis that an intervention is totally necessary, it's still possible to break up what intervention is to be taken across the proclivities of different age groups.

Baby boomers do not undertake the same activities as Gen Z, Lynx does not sell to the same men as Old Spice, this should all be clear. If this information is not immediately to hand for the government (as one might well mount the argument it shouldn't be) then there is another obvious candidate with an interest in retaining it from whom that information could be acquired per the emergency acts violating people's privacy these very governments have so enthusiastically granted themselves; private firms have clear advertising and revenue maximising interests in understanding and marketing to the demographics of their customers.

So, acquire this information and, to strike a balance between limiting viral impact and maintaining viable macroeconomic finances, project a ratio of the indexed severity which is likely to be experienced through the generations onto the correspondingly most-used firms by each of them and stratify the severity of interventions accordingly.

Presumably one would do this by in-situ sales requiring a physical outlet as opposed to online sales for obvious reasons regarding transmission in closed, congregated spaces, though other metrics can be imagined.

But no, such an approach, where thought of at all, is immediately shouted down by cries of 'discrimination!' and 'divisiveness!'. Discriminatory?

Yes, openly so and so are you.

Have you ever made any decision in your life where you have ranked the priority of two or more competing and mutually exclusive interests against one another through whatever matrix you like and then arrived at a conclusion? i.e. anything varying from what brand of biscuits you'd like with tea to which person you'd like to marry and whatever else in between you can possibly conceive (most obviously and totally and perhaps by that combination most powerfully—the definitionally exclusive choices of what you do with each unrecoverably passing second of each uncrecoverably passing day, such as reading this book)?

If yes, congratulations, you've engaged in discrimination, welcome to Earth. If no, please explain your ways to laymen like me, for you must be such a sensei of pluripotentiality that the laws of time bend to your will (Einstein would be jealous!).

Certainly, some discrimination is stupid, morally unjustifiable and deplorable: racism, sexism, etc, especially in a meritocratic system or in fact, any system which depends on the fundamental unit equity of each of its constituents to function (where these examples are most often raised). But decrying any given system simply on the grounds of 'discrimination!' rather than the key modifier: 'UNJUSTIFIED discrimination!' is to, by nature of human decision and time, decry every important decision between any number of conflicting options you've ever made in the same breath.

As to that modifier itself, I've explained the matrices for which one would come to that conclusion previously; the meta-moral debate as to whether or not they are good matrices at all would fall outside of this book's scope, no matter how much the author would love to go down that particular rabbit hole.

For the cries of division I must turn first, regrettably, to that nemesis of the scientific method, anecdote. Contain your cries of horror; the expedition shall be brief.

My experience with our local Tory apologists in our university's Forum debate on the issue of whether our government had handled COVID well saw them defend a broadstroke approach disregarding the characteristics of differing devolved areas on account of 'national unity!' It is worth noting, the antecedent breath preached about the brilliance of a testing system which used Bayesian probability (after I had to point out for them that this was in fact what their own argument consisted of) to discriminate between different areas of the country which behaved differently in response to interventions and so would need different approaches.

Two obviously contradictory thoughts.

This was the system on which the UK based its hugely unpopular tier system, but this will be discussed later. The point is next time someone raises this objection, that varying policy by age and its corresponding vulnerability to COVID, see if their *replicatio* of their overlords is ensconced in such stunning intellectual honesty and consistency. From there, draw your own conclusions.

A further interesting dive is into the exact nature of the statement. The statement itself states nothing as to death rates or to the population metrics if measured either modally, by mean, or any other measure. Simple third-party correlations could explain this instead then; countries with an older median population may have better reporting systems as they are usually more developed (an older median would be dragged out by more people living longer but also perhaps declining birth rates shrinking the younger side of the average). So it may not be a case of age exacerbating causally but a coincidence between societies which allow people to live longer shifting the median out also retaining better infrastructure to accurately monitor caseload.

Subtleties of the statement aside; it shouldn't be taken to assert any increased severity amongst the elderly in and of itself (this has and will be discussed elsewhere) the solutions aforementioned should still stand on their own.

2.   A longer time from the first report of a case in a country

to border closures correlated with an increased caseload
there compared to others who closed borders faster.

This point seems simple. People can carry viruses across borders,
this being even more the case where symptoms take some time to
manifest after infection and/or some people can be
presymptomatically infective and develop symptoms later or
asymptomatic entirely—both in the case of COVID-19.

So the correlation is observed between delayed border
closures and increased caseloads. There may also be an analysis to
be carried out between those economies more dependent on
tourism and injections from visitors which thereby have a strong
incentive to remain open and those who do not by then comparing
against both timeframe of border closures and numbers coming
into the country throughout that relevant timeframe.

The scope of this book and its intended propositions bear
bringing up here. Everybody wants reduced caseloads but its hardly
a libertarian position to go around closing borders. The relative
risk of the practice was relatively strong, second only to the prior
variable of age in correlation to caseload.

The deontological position against tightening borders in crises
is self-explanatory: imposing arbitrary rules on the free movement
of people (this includes national borders, where arbitrary is taken
to mean any practice lacking *a priori* deductive validity) and
enforcing those arbitrary rules through a manner which
definitionally invokes aggressive violence should be, *prima facie*,
morally illegitimate.

The consequential case is more complicated. We here submit
however that, especially in the case of aforementioned economies
dependent on tourism and international service markets such as
commercial flying which serve this industry, the damage done by
these policies far outstripped any utility they provided, especially
when the inherent disadvantages of the policies outside this area

are added into the analysis.

It can be fairly asserted in the author's view without any need for a statistical significance test that locking down a nation damages its income from tourism—any test would obviously pass statistical significance attempting to show it, rendering the exercise a tautology. If one wishes for a breakdown of the figures anyway, here it is:

In order to factor in the transnational factors the tourism markets and its dependent sub-markets operate in, its best to look at a global approach first. By this reckoning, tourism was responsible for some 10.4% of all global economic activity in 2018; a value of some $8.8 trillion. Multiple regional airlines have already filed for bankruptcy just in the US and UK, never mind elsewhere in the world.[44]

Tracking losses from that total emergent in a year not even complete at time of writing is more difficult to submit with any honesty. We can make some basic inductions though. Tourists from China spent $277bn abroad in the same year, so constituting 3.1% of the total expenditure.[45]

This might not seem a significant amount to a lay person in and of itself, but, for the purposes of illustration, imagine a 3.1% recession in a nation's economy in one year. Economists and mathematicians will appreciate that this metaphor does not exactly abstract because a recession is a shrinkage across an entire

[44] Quinn, C. (2020, April 1). The Tourism Industry Is in Trouble. These Countries Will Suffer the Most. *Foreign Policy*. Retrieved November 16, 2020, from:
https://foreignpolicy.com/2020/04/01/coronavirus-tourism-industry-worst-hit-countries-infographic/
[45] Uğur, N. G., & Akbıyık, A. (2020). Impacts of COVID-19 on global tourism industry: A cross-regional comparison. *Tourism Management Perspectives, 36*, 100744.
doi:10.1016/j.tmp.2020.100744

economy, rather than a simple removal of one source of demand and the figures would not translate on the same order from a microeconomic loss in one market to a macroeconomic recession but the metaphor holds for the point to be made.

A loss of that magnitude would be recoverable, as the reader can likely imagine, if that's all which occurred.

But now, for the purpose of full intellectual honesty, extend that metaphor to the point where that 3.1% recession was induced by a loss of business from one group of people within one sector, to a situation where the likely actual damage is much larger and this 3.1% is all that's currently known; the canary in the coal mine as it were.

The immediate difference in policy prescription, which should have been obvious once one realises the difference upon expanding the situation fully, is the vastly limited amount of knowledge in the full example even without any distortions by relative position.

Being fully earnest, the assumption is required here that if the complexity of the transnational tourism market, a global entity, is sufficient to require at each stage of comprehension (and therefore, in each inferential step about its nature) roughly the same amount of knowledge required per good decision as someone managing a national economy, the point holds on the epistemological grounds that managing the two is of equivalent difficulty, but managing a single economy can be centralised—a global market cannot.

In simpler words; the implication to the second degree which must follow from the previous is this: Medical advisers to and bureaucrats within governments likely had a good enough model of the consequential benefits of a lockdown to accurately understand those benefits. Even if there wasn't a prior sample size of lockdowns about which they knew enough to conduct statistical tests on the worth of the policy, Bayesian analysis could make a prediction as to the likely outcomes, wherever individual elements could not be satisfactorily tested in isolation within the scientific method.

The same *cannot* be said of the costs of such policies, due to, in the first degree, the local knowledge of those affected by these costs and in the second, the dispersed bodies over which this information, the processing of which would already be corrupted in veracity by relative position of the pertinent actors (here referring to the combination in outputs on knowledge of Hayek's Local Knowledge Problem[46] and Mises' Economic Calculation Problem,[47] expounded upon by the author here.) and how in relation to it between the pertinent actors, being just that, dispersed.

This is not to say that public health advisers are to be blamed for this, at least in any significant moral regard. The moral concerns were first of all, not their charge, at least through this vector of calculus and secondly, neither was the economics of the policy (though removing this charge was at best questionable and at worst creates this very problem). Many took advice on the economics of the position but still made clear that consideration was not their role.

Still, even where they were not the decision makers, there is an epistemological imbalance to two degrees in the advice provided to governments. The first imbalance is one of internal weighting before the advice ever left the mouths of those dispensing it; advice on public health, virology and epidemiology likely does not factor in macroeconomics, but the inverse does not hold.

Hence, a policy which favoured the former over the latter

---

[46] Friedrich A. Hayek (1945). *The Use of Knowledge*, American Economic Review. XXXV: 4. pp. 519–530.
[47] Von Mises, Ludwig, (1990). *Economic calculation in the Socialist Commonwealth* (PDF) Mises Institute.

could, and, given the pressures on time for administrations to decide quickly on a course of action, likely would be granted undue weight when formulated by those criteria pursuant to the relationship between them on account of this imbalance.

Then, there is an external imbalance. This occurred when decision makers, not being aware of the first imbalance, failed to correct for it in their thinking and pursuant decisions on policy. This then exaggerates the first error by whatever degree those decision makers further held the priority of: 'public health > public credit', as there is self-evident political incentive to do.

3. Increased numbers of cases per million correlated with rates of obesity

Discussing any topic which so much as implies any negative consequences of obesity or unhealthy levels of fat in the body is enough to get you ostracised in some areas of modern media. We can thank the 'fat acceptance movement', aided and abetted in their collective delusion by the mainstream media, for this.

They do have one point; people should not be discriminated against on account of their body in most theatres of life, but this standing as a general rule doesn't magically make fat healthy nor critique of that belief 'fatphobia' to be censored.

To lay the background out, obesity, where defined as a BMI greater than 30kg per square metre, has a long and replicable history of increasing co-morbidity risks of other health risks; being obese increases the risk that you die compared to a person who is not when presented with the same phenomenon, bar obvious exemptions like starvation.

An NCBI study on its effects, admittedly applying more to the United States than Europe specifically, published some 10 years ago which outlines its health effects generally.[48]

McTigue's et.al.'s study in 2006 shows the rates for obese adults raised for mortality at an additional 23% on top of the control group.[49] This factor can be dispensed with relatively quickly, just as Chaudhry et. al.'s study does—assuming that obesity increases morbidity generally, you'd expect to see this correlation here.

Perhaps the most remarkable aspect isn't its emergence but the strength of the correlation compared to the others phenomena measured—the second strongest correlator in cases per million in Chaudhry et. al.'s study.

This is more evidence on the pile, yet more for the delusional to deny.

4. Nations with higher GDP per capita (PPP) correlated with a higher rate of morbidity and critical illness

This is another one which seems counter-intuitive. Surely one would expect nations with a lower GDP per capita and therefore likely less development per other indices like the Human Development Index (HDI) or any other one wishes to use, would show more severe results on account of a less capable healthcare system?

Chaudhry's study doesn't speculate or invite discussion as to why this might be the case. The author's limited knowledge of the biology might be enough to make a few inductions. COVID-19 seems to be a virus passed primarily by respiratory processes and

---

[48] Pi-Sunyer, X. (2010). The Medical Risks of Obesity. *NCBI.* doi:10.3897/bdj.4.e7720.figure2f

[49] McTigue K, Larson JC, Valoski A, et al. Mortality and cardiac and vascular outcomes in extremely obese women. JAMA. 2006;296(1):79-86.

proximity to those infected through those processes. It is true that nations with a higher average GDP per capita have a loose correlation to higher population density; there are stronger correlations with population density such as geographic location on the globe.[50]

So if this is the case, part of the explanation might be people living in closer together in nations with a higher GDP per capita which increases infection, but this doesn't answer the precise correlation which was rather with criticality and morbidity than caseload. Other than that, I come up empty – I invite you dear reader, to go elsewhere for a more complete picture of this phenomenon as it is investigated.

5. Reduced income dispersion was associated with reduced criticality of cases

It is notable that income dispersion has relationships with one of the previous criteria used—GDP per capita. Brueckner and Lederman's 2017 paper found econometric links between GDP per capita and income inequality which varied depending on the initial income of the nation in question:

> *Instrumental variables estimates suggest that inequality has a negative effect on aggregate output for the median country with a 2015 PPP GDP per capita of around 10000USD. For Low Income Countries, income inequality has a positive effect on GDP per capita. The paper documented that the relationship between inequality and human capital*

---

[50] University of Oxford. (2017). *GDP per capita vs population density, 2017.* Retrieved November 21, 2020, from:
https://ourworldindata.org/grapher/population-density-vs-prosperity.

is significantly decreasing in countries' initial incomes. Overall, the empirical results provide support for the hypothesis that income inequality is beneficial for transitional growth in poor countries but that it is detrimental for growth in high-income economies.[51]

The question then follows as to why they were used separately rather than indexed together or in conjunction with another index.

Chaudhry et.al. gives the following justification: 'Our interest in including the Gini Index was to see if high levels of systemic corruption in the flow of goods and services within a nation impact the risk of COVID-19 related death and other clinical outcomes.'

They later go on to mention the Corruption Perceptions Index, collect and present data for it, yet mention it nowhere in the abstract or initial discussion. I, and I'm sure many others, will agree that conflating a measure of income inequality with 'systemic corruption', no matter any correlation between income inequality and corruption does the credibility of the study great damage to those who read it sufficiently carefully—I cannot see an alternative explanation where Gini-indexed income inequality, the index they use, was included as a contrasting measure of corruption to the eponymous index in any sincere or accurate way.

Conflation at best, or deliberate misdirection at worst, seems to be the best probabilistic explanation here.

On the observation itself, one possibility may be that local markets operating on a basis with less capacity for demand

---

[51] Brueckner, M., & Lederman, D. (2017, September). *Inequality and GDP per capita: The Role of Initial Income* [Scholarly project]. In *World Bank*. Retrieved November 21, 2020, from: http://pubdocs.worldbank.org/en/755201504498011731/inequality-and-growth-3-september-2017.pdf

stratification by price, due to greater income equality, allow greater access to their goods and services as a result of price discrimination becoming a less effective strategy.

It follows that perhaps there is greater access to healthcare utility per unit of currency in local markets operating on that basis. Another might be a simple correlation between states with a progressive tax system which increases income equality also places greater emphasis on healthcare access than those which do not, hence mitigating cases before they advance to the critical stage or beyond. Whatever the case, the observation itself seems to remain factually valid *prima facie* despite the unfortunate choices used to demonstrate it.

Assuming a sound methodology, the discussion section becomes particularly useful. Testing regimes for the virus were often made an issue of special political bleating in many countries; you'll remember the criticism of the Swedish PM on these grounds previously. Testing regimes were put into place by the countries throughout Europe at varying points where at all, per Figure 4, taken from the BBC website, originally computed from ECDC data: [52]

---

[52] Kovacevic, T., & Butcher, B. (2020, October 9). *Covid in Europe: How much testing do other countries do?* BBC. Retrieved October 20, 2020, from https://www.bbc.co.uk/news/54181291

Overall tests by country

Anitgen tests carried out by selected European country between 9 March and 20 September

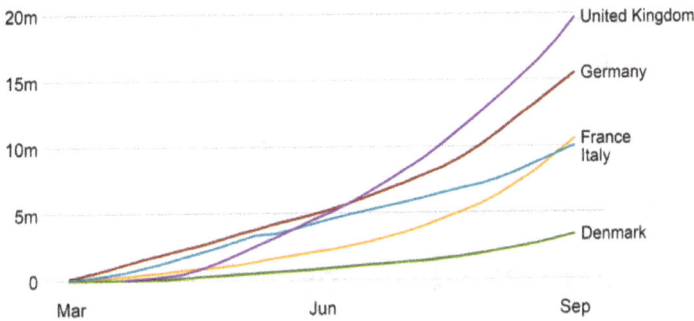

Figure 4

A graph to show total tests for COVID-19 conducted by different nations across the months of March-September

This is an incomplete graph of course when seeking to describe all of Europe—full data from the ECDC can be found here.[53]

All this varying information might suggest that the data is out on how strictly testing regimens correlate to reduced damage from the virus. This doesn't necessarily imply any causal relationship (or the lack thereof) between testing regimens and outcomes; it's worth remembering the old adage that correlation is not causation.

Testing was not associated significantly with reductions in mortality or critical cases.

Indeed, testing being inferred to have any relationship to outcomes may be a fallacious conclusion in and of itself; the discussion section addresses the correlation between a higher GDP per capita scaling with increased reporting of critical cases and

---

[53] *Weekly surveillance summary.* (2020, October 15). Retrieved October 20, 2020, from:
https://covid19-country-overviews.ecdc.europa.eu/#33_sweden.

deaths: 'Countries with a higher per capita GDP had an increased number of reported critical cases and deaths per million population.

This may reflect more widespread testing in those countries, greater transparency with reporting and better national surveillance systems.'

In short, it may not be correct to assume that all testing strategies are comparable, or that testing rates and coverage are constant across all concerned countries.

European Politics and Vaccine Supranationalism

Enough abstract studying! I apologise if the last chapter might have seemed a tad out of place, but rejoice, we can move back to the red meat of shredding politicians. The specific European context offers replete opportunity.

First, let us look to its handling of vaccinations.

At the onset of the pandemic, it was presumed by many that, against the UK which had dared defy Brussels and finally finished up Brexit, the EU would triumph in protecting its citizens and further make itself the exemplar of virtue Remainers would have you believe it is.

Oh. Ohohohoho.

Oh, how the Remainers laughed and guffawed about how their star-frisbee waving overlords would have their moment of supremacy. But how they were force fed humble pie for breakfast, lunch and dinner by the actions of one of their own, one Ursula von der Leyen.

For those unfamiliar, our Little Mermaid antagonist has apparently taken up a side-hustle as a German politician; most recently as President of the European Commission since the 1st of December 2019. Highlights include being in Time's 100 Most

Influential for 2020, Angela Merkel's Minister of Defence, and the inceptor of vaccine nationalism in Europe.

This policy came about in response to considerable latency from her own side. There were points where the UK's % of population vaccinated outweighed the EU's by some 3:1. This came about for a variety of reasons. First of all, the EMA approved the use of the Oxford AstraZeneca Vaccine in January of 2021. However, some member states refused to deploy it for citizens over age 65. This issue worsened on the 7th of April when, after initially denying any link between the AstraZeneca vaccine and lethal blood clots, the EMA revised its position and stated that there was a possible link.

The UK still proudly flew the flag of the vaccine (consequentialists would argue correctly so; one is more likely to die of a lightning strike than AstraZeneca vaccine induced blood clot) and only recommended that some other vaccine be used where possible for under 30's and that, if not, AstraZeneca should still be used. Not so in Europe.

The Dutch bailed first, abandoning their oft-cited courage though only stopping its deployment for the aged. Some which followed did so more dramatically, with Denmark ceasing its rollout altogether. Shorters on AstraZeneca's stock popped open the champagne and public opinion tanked, with minorities of both French and German voters thinking well of the AstraZeneca vaccine.

One might, in a model of right-wing meritocracy der Leyen's party is supposed to back, take responsibility for these issues and solve them. You might especially think this given that, in what was touted as a display of unity at the time, all remaining member states signed up to a plan transferring responsibility for vaccine acquisition out of their own national sovereignty and into Brussels.

Instead of taking responsibility for the conflicting policies of members and the inability to persuade their own citizens to take up a vaccine, EU leaders with her at the helm, decided to throw a hissy-fit in an attempt to get their way. You see, some 10.9M vaccines had been exported from the EU to the UK, as the UK's contracts with AstraZeneca and other vaccine suppliers needed distributing and importing from outside production.

EU leaders were furious about the lack of vaccines (which they can't get their own people to take) coming back the other way, and so decided to, by their own standards, play God with the lives of British citizens and discussed the idea of an export ban from the EU. Continental System 2, Electric Boogaloo, it was to be.

This, thankfully, didn't stand and was struck down prior to passage, and the toddler self-identifying as a Commission instead demanded transparency from the UK in terms of its vaccine policy and that AstraZeneca deliver on its contractual obligations with the EU faster.

So, instead it was: 'Transparency for thee but not me, especially where finances are concerned. Also, any firms which contract with us should be prepared for us to, by our own standards, kill civilians who were five short years ago our very own by interference should we not like how you choose to execute your contracts, even if the contract in question predates our own.'

What icons of morality.

What fitting behaviour from the best arbiters of sound decision making since sliced bread, at least, if one remembers the Remain campaign's branding of the Fourth Reich.

It could have ended there. What would have been, in any other time, a diplomatic *faux pas* to crown them all, if not an outright consideration of trade war, could have been the end of this sick comedy of errors. Oh no. The Concert had only smashed up the piano and drums—the brassists, stringers and woodwinders yet lived! So more was the order of the day.

The EU's other partners saw problems with production and

deployment. Some others have not even passed clinical trials as of the time of writing. All credit to Ursula, she did publicly recognise this wrong and the surrounding mistakes. The rules surrounding the federalised vaccine buyout scheme are much simpler than the language they are written in and surrounding discussion might imply. It effectively combines a degree of autonomy whilst placing the EU itself as buyer *primus inter pares*—EU members can make their own deals with vaccine companies with which the EU has not negotiated and arrived at a deal.

With companies where it has, no deal. Despite this, Germany made a separate order with Pfizer in September for some 30M extra vaccines. The Commission predictably refused to say one way or tother on whether this violated the terms of the agreement...

Irrespective of internal tensions, EU members initiated orders from elsewhere. France and Germany discussed the possibility of co-operating with Russia, whilst Hungary and Slovakia went ahead and bought into Sputnik directly. Austria, Denmark and Israel took an approach looking forward, stating that they would work jointly on a second generation of vaccines designed to address different mutations COVID might undergo—this despite vaccine producers in the first generation claiming that their vaccines would handle all the different strains of COVID.

This tied into the second way COVID affected European politics—it showed the EU's willingness to use teeth, but also affected politics on the national level of member states.

The example which should immediately leap to mind is Hungary. Potential correlations between infectious diseases and authoritarian politics will be discussed more fully later, but if one was to find an immediately obvious anchor, Hungary may be a good choice.

The Hungarian government managed to conceal their actions by joining a statement put out by 16 other members reaffirming the power of the Commission to uphold the rule of law and other protections. The statement didn't explicitly mention Hungary, but there was no other possible intended target implied at the time. The action in question the Hungarian Government granting itself plenary power (unlimited power to deal with a certain crisis within its own borders, think Enabling Act) by a qualified majority in its Parliament. German Minister for State Michael Roth was the only one to show any spine, suggesting the immediate deployment of economic sanctions to turn the Hungarian Government back from this course.

Der Leyen simply recommended that the legislation in question be confined to its stated purpose—because that's how these acts have been used, always and without deviation, of course...

Escalations from that stage forward seem to have been rather phony. Thirteen party leaders made proposals to the European federation of centre-right parties, the EPP, to expunge the ruling Hungarian party, Fidesz. Leader Viktor Orban simply replied that he was happy to discuss the membership of his party once the pandemic is over. Despite this, the National Assembly declared the national emergency to be resolved on June 16. You might be asking 'What's the harm?'

The answer is simple—the EU has now permitted member states to rule by decree where they deem an emergency sufficiently severe. A precedent has been set and the incentive now exists—should one desire imperial power, simply manufacture a crisis sufficiently serious to invoke rule by decree, and profit from there.

Yet more organs of the EU fell to coerced censorship. The European External Action Service (EEAS), began with a mandate to combat mis- and dis-information on the pandemic, chiefly from China and Russia. It failed even in this, and we only know due to a leaker who immediately had an investigation ordered against them. Original reports made multiple allegations. Chiefly these were that:

'[the CCP was promoting] unproven theories about the origin of COVID-19', '[China was unduly emphasising] displays of gratitude by some European leaders in response to Chinese aid' and that this was part of a 'continued and coordinated push by official Chinese sources to deflect any blame.'[54]

Then, the New York Times broke a corresponding different story;[55] that the report had been amended to the substantially less damning: 'We see a continued and coordinated push by some actors, including Chinese sources, to deflect any blame'. This had been permitted by the intervention of one Josep Borrell, High Representative of the EU, who delayed the report under coercion from Chinese authorities, according to the leak. Borrell's response? To order an investigation into the leak...[56]

Such accountability.

A befittingly low response from such a 'high' office.

Finally, one might conclude that the pandemic has laid low any illusion of 'European solidarity'. The Serbian President himself called European solidarity 'a fairy tale'.[57] This can be seen most

---

[54] *EU toned down Chinese disinformation report after it threatened "repercussions."* (2020, April 25). South China Morning Post. https://www.scmp.com/news/china/diplomacy/article/3081564/eu-toned-down-report-chinese-disinformation-after-beijing

[55] Apuzzo, M. (2020, April 24). *Pressured by China, E.U. Softens Report on Covid-19 Disinformation.* The New York Times. https://www.nytimes.com/2020/04/24/world/europe/disinformation-china-eu-coronavirus.html

[56] von der Burchard, H. (2020, May 27). *EU's diplomatic service launches probe over China disinformation leak.* POLITICO. https://www.politico.eu/article/eus-diplomatic-service-investigates-leak-on-china-disinformation-report/

[57] *Serbian President Labels European Solidarity "Fairy Tale",* (n.d.). British Virgin Islands. https://bvi.org/serbian-president-labels-european-solidarity-fairy-tale-says-only-china-can-assist-in-coronavirus-

clearly in the bloc's response to Italy; if the EU as a whole took an uppercut from COVID, Italy got knocked out of the ring.

By November 2020, cases were confirmed to have reached 1.6M, some 2.6% of the population by most estimates, but remember that the real number is almost certainly greater. Lockdowns and following damage to finances caused a 7% shrinkage in GDP but, most importantly, a rise in debt to GDP ratio from an already eye-watering 130% to 155%.[58]

The 12 March Black Thursday hit the Italian stock market nearly hardest of all; the FTSE MIB lost 17% of its value in 24 hours.[59]

So it was that, on the 25th of March Italy, along with multiple other members, penned a joint letter to the Council of Europe, advocating for a new kind of response. There would be a 'eurobond' or 'coronabond' which would be bought into so as to ride out the coming economic recession and reward those who placed faith in the ability of the states concerned to respond profitably once the pandemic waned.

Crucially, it would be a common debt mechanism, loading equally across the bloc. The proposal was met with opposition from the Netherlands and, you guessed it, Germany.

Fair play from their point of view; these two are amongst the most financially solvent and strongest creditors, with the most to

response
[58] ISTAT), N. I. of S. (2019, May 10). Italy Government Debt to GDP. Tradingeconomics.com; TRADING ECONOMICS.
https://tradingeconomics.com/italy/government-debt-to-gdp
[59] Allen, V. Z., Nathan. (2020, March 13). *Italy, Spain curb trading to stem coronavirus market crash.* Reuters.
https://www.reuters.com/article/us-europe-stocks-short-selling/italy-spain-curb-trading-to-stem-coronavirus-market-crash-idUSKBN2101LN

lose by having their comparative financial advantage erased. After two further meetings of the Eurogroup, the possibility of using the ESM system out of Luxembourg, but that there would be no new financial vehicle.

Conclusions on Europe

So, what is to be drawn from the European approach to COVID wrote whole?

Firstly, that German supremacy within the union has been confirmed in stronger terms than ever before, especially now that it lacks the UK as a counterbalance. However, those who could be convinced of that likely already were in 2016, and those who were not, will not be.

More incisive as to immediate political developments is the EU's seemingly paradoxical ability to play host to both nationalism within its borders and supranationalism to those outside of its borders. Hungarian nationalism as discussed was at play for the world to see throughout the crisis, yet the EU took no credible action.

Since reviewing this chapter, both France[60] and Italy[61] have seen fit to enact vaccine passport schemes within their own borders, with the French deployment coinciding with notably increased nationalist rhetoric by Macron. Watching Marine Le Pen

---

[60] Sage, A. (2021, August 8). *Macron defiant after mass protests over French vaccine passports.* Thetimes.co.uk; The Times. https://www.thetimes.co.uk/article/macron-defiant-after-mass-protests-over-french-vaccine-passports-mbxcb2360

[61] Adams, C. (2021, July 23). *Italy introduces vaccine passports for indoor activities.* The Independent. https://www.independent.co.uk/travel/news-and-advice/italy-vaccine-passport-covid-delta-restaurants-b1889194.html

defend freedom of religion over the Macron regime on live television was surreal.

Despite all this, the Union has done nothing.

Yet despite this, bureaucrats like Von Der Leyen are more than happily playing a game of supranationalism with actors outside the bloc, requiring pretension to ignorance of the very same prior division within its borders.

The lesson from this contradiction as it applies to your own praxis may not be immediately obvious, so to spell it out, it is that politicians will only react against inconsistencies where they have incentive to do so, and will more than happily defend mutually irreconcilable positions if it is profitable to do so.

As such, it is the duty of every citizen to deduce the truth and demand that their politicians act accordingly, if that truth is to be protected across all strata of political power.

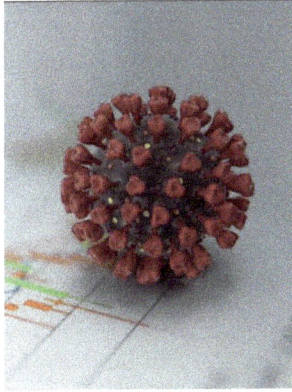

Section 4—COVID-1984 in the United States, the Land of the Slave and the Home of the Fee

Do not practice what you do not want to become.
—Jordan B. Peterson

Those that can give up essential liberty to gain a little temporary safety deserve neither liberty nor safety.
—Benjamin Franklin

Politics

THE TWIN ASSERTIONS of this chapter are simple.

First, COVID-19 ended the Trump Presidency. It's also the reason why Joe Biden is Number 46. There may have been other factors, such as the Democrats selecting a candidate who was actually electable to run their ticket as opposed to 2016.

The BLM protests which swept across the nation prior to the election and subsequent heavy-handed response to them no doubt damaged the Trump campaign further. Another factor may have been especially memorable gaffes like being the healthiest President there ever was.[62]

But more than anything else, COVID-19, and the actions taken to stop it, specifically the economic consequences of those actions, was what decided the outcome.

Second, it will also prove to be the prime determinant of at least the first year of the Biden administration, and so far, it is being scapegoated more than it is managed.

Though the Biden regime has arguably so far been in mid-2021 been beset by crisis without end, the current state of play seems to be that it is naught but a poor man's Second Carter Administration.

The Prelude

The Trump campaigns generally, but especially in 2020, outside of the cultish and nationalistic MAGA appeal, seemed to be appealing to swing voters by turning the election into a referendum on the economy.

Hardly a seductive political talking point for one's aesthetic taste but ultimately what rationally talks and an effective strategy if one believes that the necessary pluralities will vote accordingly if convinced.

This could be said of any strategy but you get the point of the

[62] Brait, E. (2015, December 14). *Donald Trump would be America's healthiest President, doctor's letter says.* The Guardian. Retrieved December 13, 2020, from https://www.theguardian.com/us-news/2015/dec/14/donald-trump-health-doctor-letter-americas-healthiest-president

dichotomy; It's the economy, stupid!'

Such a topic would have been especially useful for a President—both Republican and incumbent—discussing relatively well sanitised topics compared to his 2016 run would keep turnout low, favouring Republicans broadly, and it stands at least to my instinctive assertion that incumbents would benefit from calmer campaigns, due to the ultimately larger share of attention the person in the White House is going to get courtesy of already having a track record, familiarity with the public and any narrative being told, alongside the most to lose, this further amplified by the reputation Trump had already built for himself one way or another.

Prior to COVID-19, it also seemed one where Trump would have been well placed to win a second term with healthy economic growth coinciding with his Presidency prior to the virus emerging; that term carefully selected on account of the disagreement as to what actually generated that growth.

Whilst that discussion is interesting on its own count, further discussion of Obama hangover into Trumponomics would be outside the purview of this book.

The Biden campaign decided to run a countering narrative; they sought from the outset to cast the election as a referendum on Trump's character.

This, for what should have been manifestly obvious reasons given the nation burning throughout the campaign, would hand them an easy victory.

Though such times are often correctly held by the more distant to be that when economic thought should be given highest weight, it is not what will be on the mind of the general populace. Give them the cocaine that is an easily castigated scapegoat to blame and watch the fireworks.

It is far more cathartic and commanding of a deeper moral imperative to speak of grand ideas and issues of morality rather than spreadsheets.

This remains true no matter one's intention (or lack thereof) to actually follow through on that difference, where any differences are more than skin deep in the first place in the U.S. political system, even assuming any complete understanding of these differences on the part of the campaigners.

Taking a deeper look at why this strategy was so vital to the Trump campaign and was so undermined by its candidates' own actions, let's take a look at a few graphs to show.

Real GDP Growth Relative to Pre–November 2016 Projections

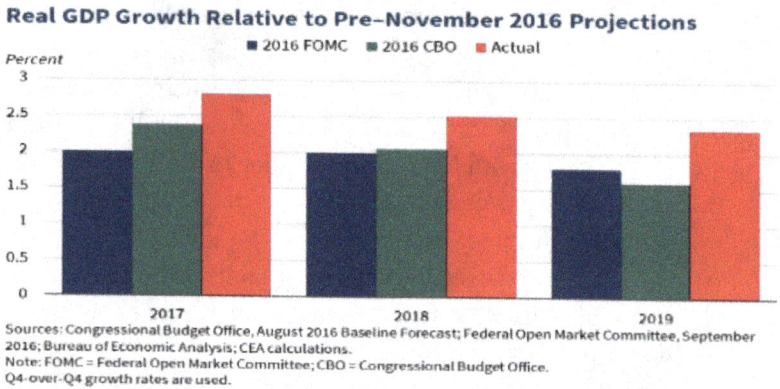

Sources: Congressional Budget Office, August 2016 Baseline Forecast; Federal Open Market Committee, September 2016; Bureau of Economic Analysis; CEA calculations.
Note: FOMC = Federal Open Market Committee; CBO = Congressional Budget Office.
Q4-over-Q4 growth rates are used.

Figure 4 (above)[63] shows Real GDP growth in red (GDP growth corrected for inflation) against predictions in 2016 from both the Congressional Budget Office in green and the Federal Open Market Committee in blue. We can clearly see that real growth exceeded all predictions ahead of time; Trump did better than he

---

[63] Council of Economic Advisors. (2020, January 30). *WhiteHouse.gov* (United States, White House, Executive). Retrieved December 13, 2020, from:
https://www.whitehouse.gov/articles/united-states-gdp-growth-continues-exceeding-expectations/

was expected to when elected prior to COVID-19's onset.

One can also mount an international comparison of US GDP growth against other countries, say, the G7:

Annualized U.S. Real GDP Growth vs. Other G7 Countries Since 2016 Election

Percent

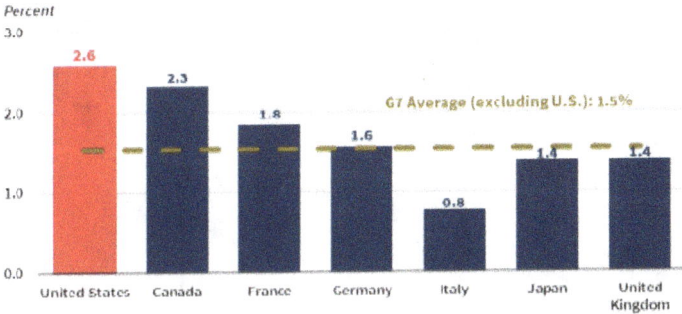

Sources: Various national statistical offices; CEA calculations.
Note: Values represent growth at a compound annual rate from 2016:Q4 through 2019:Q3.

Figure 5 (above) shows U.S. Real GDP growth in red against all other members of the G7 in blue since the 2016 election.

U.S. growth during this period is the highest on the table. Some might call it protectionism, but, if one is running a political calculus on the basis of economics, re-election signs would have looked good at the time.

I'm not suddenly mounting a general defence of protectionism—the free marketeers have the point in my view that extending it out over the long run causes a net loss—but politicians never needed things to work in the long run provided they can sell a campaign to people obsessed with image on the correct emotion.

GDP was not the only indicator on the upswing; the BBC did a good job compiling some others for those who decry GDP as an accurate economic indicator for people generally.

The Dow Jones Index grew much faster under Trump before COVID than it ever did during the Obama years as per Figure 6 (below): [64]

Stock market growth and jitters: The Dow Jones index

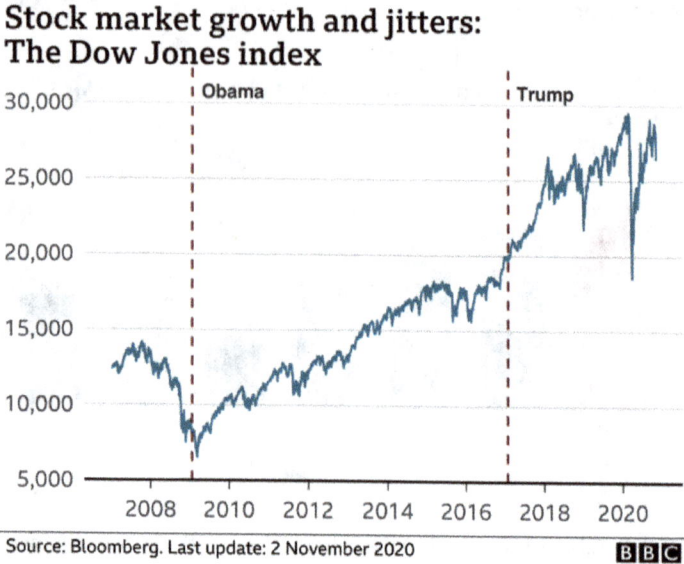

Source: Bloomberg. Last update: 2 November 2020

BBC

Figure 6

Unemployment continued to fall, reaching the lowest levels in half a century, at least, until COVID, as demonstrated by Figure 7 (below):

---

[64] Check, R. (2020, November 3). US 2020 election: The economy under Trump in six charts. *BBC*. Retrieved December 13, 2020, from https://www.bbc.co.uk/news/world-45827430

Unemployment rate continues to fall after April high
Percentage of US labour force not in work

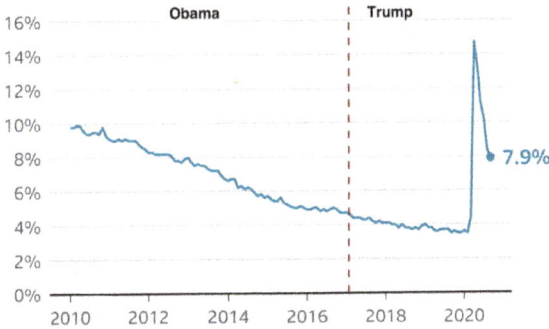

Figure 7

Real wages continued increasing steadily, briefly thrown into flux by COVID but normalising out by August as shown by Figure 8 (below):

Wages wobble but continue to rise
Average hourly earnings, dollars per hour, adjusted for inflation

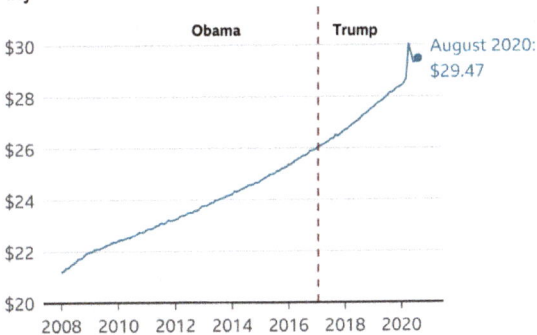

Figure 8

Finally, poverty is in an interesting vector to compare through.

It's reduction is not an image one necessarily associates with the fatcat corporatists of the Trump regime, but statistics might tell you a different story. Figures for 2020 are not available as of the time of writing but anyone can guess the consequence of the pandemic; either it's going to increase or the rate of its decrease is going to slow.

Take a look at Figure 9 (below):

Poverty rate in 2019 at an all time low

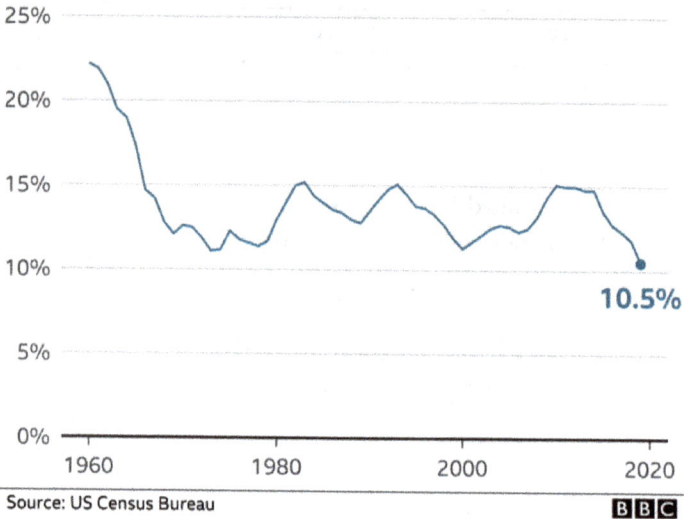

Source: US Census Bureau

Figure 9

Poverty decreased to an all-time low during the Trump administration in 2019 on a percentage measure, though it was not the year in which the largest number of Americans were lifted out of poverty as the then-President claimed; that honour (one of his few) goes to LBJ in 1966.[65]

All this was firmly going the way of the Trump administration prior to the onset of COVID. So it may have made sense at the time to run an electoral strategy based on the idea of 'vote for us and your wallet will thank you', especially when 'Crooked Joe' was never going to work as well as 'Crooked Hilary'. This couldn't hold on however, when the actions taken by the Trump administration in response to the onset of COVID so undermined this prior success.

How Trump's Morally Grey Appeal was lost to COVID

It remains the author's thesis that a large part of Trump's appeal heading into the 2016 election was his morally grey nature.

This is not to say that his opponents were any more or less so, but as politics as a wider whole gradually became more identitarian, it became increasingly necessary to brand the identity of candidates in an appealing way, or, where this was impossible, miniaturise, mitigate and distract.

So it was that the Trump branding focused on Making America Great Again as a collective entity and goal, more than happy to rant on about the modern failings of character (arguments which bear merit) but conveniently dodging any reference to the character of its own forebear.

Wherever accusations of illegal rent discrimination practices or treatment of women were posed as material for impeachment

---

[65] Census Bureau. (2020). *Poverty Data Tables* (United States, Census Bureau, Department of Commerce). Retrieved December 13, 2020, from:
https://www.census.gov/topics/income-poverty/poverty/data/tables.1966.html

or wider moral condemnation,[66] the rebranding in question was more one of the amoral *Ubermensch*, at least, that's the view taken from across the pond here which seems to best fit the evidence.

That is to say, the appeal projected was that of a man who is so driven and consumed by his own ambition that morals become seconded to it; this would be the rule applied to the U.S. through his Presidency and by that rule, its denizens would benefit over others. In the case that citizens should worry about the rights and the rule of law being thrown in front of the populist bus, as they were right to in this instance given Trump's reaction to those on his own side over bump stocks ('Take the guns first, due process second),[67] surely the Constitution, the magical, idolised, false god of the American system would protect them?

Surely, the already imperial Supreme Court, reduced to little more than a political football by both campaigns, but especially the Democrats and their open discussion of 'court packing' (or as we more honestly call things over here, political manipulation of the judiciary) would act impartially to protect the rights of citizens, despite refusing to hear the case challenging the bump stock action, called *Guedes v BATFE*, three times in a row?

In a strange paradox, a court rendered far stronger in the legal process by *Marbury v Madison* than it was ever meant to be, simultaneously turned into naught but a vassal of *realpolitik* by rampant identitarianism which cares only for mob rule and nought for the judicial process, but this is the paradox we find ourselves in nonetheless.

When the Daily Mail attempted something similar in the UK

---

[66] Lichtman, A. *The Case for Impeachment*. William Collins.

[67] Staff, R. (2021). Fact check: Trump quote on guns misattributed to Kamala Harris. *Reuters*. Retrieved from:
https://www.reuters.com/article/uk-factcheck-trump-quote-misattribute-ka-idUSKCN26D1UI

there was uproar, yet we are to believe that America still stands as a bastion of liberty? Many statists argue that there is scant value to liberty being advocated for elsewhere on account of the shadow Lady Columbia casts around the world, despite that shadow being, after some quarter-millennium of near continually expanding statism and conflict, one of her rotting, maggot-infested corpse.

This populist image in turn helped exempt the protectionist anti-free market policies brought to a party which supposedly champions the free market and not corrupting market signals.

Calvin Coolidge would weep, but he is gone, so I shall in his place.

It also sheds an interesting light on some of his more authoritarian remarks towards both sides of the aisle: the 'Because you'd be in jail' applause light on Clinton during the Second Presidential debate leaps to mind.[68] An amoral *Ubermensch*[69] may be forgiven by some plurality of the population or in some cases even a majority, despite perception elsewhere. For other examples one can look to Genghis Khan, Napoleon, Caesar, etc.

This is not to compare the achievements of such men to Trump but because, archetypally at least, the *Ubermensch* is not cognizant of morality in his decisions (or at most, only as far as it can be used as a tool to his own ends) and as such, he would most likely believe (if not outright argue), is not subject to it, at least internally.

His supporters inherit this mindset and exempt both him and themselves from deontological judgment in their own minds; the only metric of judgment in their view is the success or failure of their enterprise as it manifests in reality. Hence the crippling inability of left-wing SJW's and MAGA supporters to converse—

---

[68] *Because You'd Be In Jail.* Youtube.com. (2021). Retrieved 4 June 2021, from https://www.youtube.com/watch?v=AFGiZT-MnI4.

[69] Nietzsche, F. Thus spoke Zarathustra

they are not just afraid of each other's possible recourse to the law or some other incarnation of force against the other on account of the strength and exclusivity of their belief systems to outsiders.

They are each acting through incompatible moral matrices which supersede a specific instance of a given discussion. There is no conversation where there can be no comparison.

Furthermore, one person and a wider community constituted of those people may judge him by the tenets of a morality to which he does not subscribe, but that has no inherent meaning to him beyond the consequences that judgment effects—morality loses internal meaning in the case of the *Ubermensch*.

The only thing with internal meaning would be an ability to stand against his ambition or question the validity of the identity in and of itself. Extrapolating this onto the United States, the choice being put to voters by the Trump campaign on the point of moral fallibility could effectively be reframed as: 'You can ask questions and lose or not ask them and win. Choose.'

This is not to say that Clinton (or Biden) campaigned honestly or that contributions to left-wing identitarianism do any good—the author is simply seeking to elucidate the characteristics of the Trump campaign and its cultish characteristics, so that we can better understand why the administration's COVID response in turn undermined its own appeal.

The problem which ended up manifesting by this approach was that, by turning the election into a referendum on the economy and creating a personal brand which depended on personal success streaming down to the rest of the populace in order to exempt deliberate moral failing, Trump 2020 became a one-trick pony.

The second GDP growth, or whatever other indicator was being Goodhart-ed[70] went the wrong way, the campaign was, in

---

[70] Goodhart, C. (2021). *Problems of Monetary Management: The UK*

polite language, scuppered.

This of course, was precisely what the Trump Presidency achieved with lockdowns and its wider COVID response in its final year; the destruction of its own campaign material, and, in a truly ironic twist, the justification of the authoritarian policies his opponent would continue to deploy and defend.

Not that Trump ever cared about freedom either, just that he was exceeded even in his authoritarian ideal by a far more softly spoken adversary. It is important to note that there were some signs of an impending recession before anybody knew of COVID—most notably an inversion of the US yield curve.[71]

This, for those unaware, is a graph which plots the yield in % rates (interest rates) of certain instruments across time and draws a line to connect those points.

Hence, an inversion of the line is an indication that recession may be imminent as longer term yields have fallen below short term yields in value—investors are therefore demanding more return in exchange for shorter term investments than long ones, contrary to orthodox understanding of risk (that it compounds over time) and following reward, due to a lack of confidence in the immediate state of the economy.

A recession follows to correct this, eliminating malinvestments which are distorting confidence in the economy alongside its overall risk profile, and the yield curve (hopefully) reverts.

Experience. SpringerLink. Retrieved 9 June 2021, from http://link.springer.com/chapter/10.1007%2F978-1-349-17295-5_4.
[71] Winck, B. (2021). The US yield curve is inverted. Here's what that means, and what the implications are for the American economy. *Business Insider.* Retrieved 4 June 2021, from https://www.businessinsider.co.za/yield-curve-inversion-explained-what-it-is-what-it-means-2019-8?r=US&IR=T.

Arturo Estrella and Frederic Mishkin[72] have continued invaluable work alongside by Campbell Harvey[73] which showed that prior inversions of yield curves accurately predicted recessions in the U.S.

However, though a recession may have been coming down the tubes, without the Trump administration's COVID response, it wouldn't have been anywhere near as the trainwreck which dominated 2020.

To give a short factual rundown of the immediate aftermath of the Trump Administration's COVID response from the Congressional Budget Office: [74]

- The unemployment rate increased from 3.5% in February to 14.7% in April—an increase of over 1 in 10 people—more than enough to sway a marginal election if employment is a prime voter issue.
- The largest of these losses occurred in industries reliant on personal interaction. Think education, hospitality and retail. These groups largely intersect with the income level most likely to be a swinging voter, another blow to the Trump campaign.
- Real consumer spending fell 17% from February to April. Tightening belts never sell well.
- Real GDP was forecast to fall at a nearly 38% annual rate

---

[72] Mishkin, F., & Estrella, A. (2000). *The Yield Curve as a Predictor of U.S. Recessions.* SSRN Electronic Journal.
https://doi.org/10.2139/ssrn.249992
[73] Harvey, C. (2021). *The Yield Curve Has Inverted. Here's Why That Matters.* Retrieved 4 June 2021, from:
https://www.fuqua.duke.edu/duke-fuqua-insights/harvey-yield-curve-2019.
[74] Congressional Budget Office. (2020). *An Analysis of the President's 2020 Budget.*

in the second quarter, or 11.2% versus the prior quarter, with a return to positive quarter-to-quarter growth of 5.0% in Q3 and 2.5% in Q4 2020. However, real GDP was not expected to regain its Q4 2019 level until 2022 or later.

- The unemployment rate was forecast to average 11.5% in 2020 and 9.3% in 2021, so rapid re-employment was not likely coming. This wasn't a sneeze which could just be swept under the rug.

So, the Trump regime made the election a referendum on the economy. They turned away moral failings with promises of financial improvements for everyday Americans.

Then, it torpedoed that very economy and watched it sink. That would have been bad enough, that pre-existing faults would have been merely made worse.

If only…

The Trump Administration's Response to COVID-19 More Broadly

The Centre for Disease Control (CDC) first warned the American public about the possibility of a local outbreak of COVID-19 on February 25th, 2020.[75]

The WHO first declared a global pandemic on March 11th and an Oval Office address was made on the same day. All travel

---

[75] Taylor, M. (2020, March 23). *Exclusive: U.S. axed CDC expert job in China months before virus outbreak. Reuters.* Retrieved December 16, 2020, from: https://www.reuters.com/article/us-health-coronavirus-china-cdc-exclusiv/exclusive-u-s-axed-cdc-expert-job-in-china-months-before-virus-outbreak-idUSKBN21910S

from Europe bar the UK was banned from 30 days. On March 28th the administration briefly floated the idea of an internal travel ban from New York, New Jersey and Connecticut in order to prevent transmission elsewhere, but this was passed up in exchange for non-binding advice after fierce gubernatorial criticism.[76]

After the initial roll-outs of stay-at-home orders of the majority of states, the Trump administration quickly reverted back to a policy of reopening the economy; the initial federal limitations were branded as "15 days to Slow the Spread." [77]

The initial aim was for April 12th to mark the reopening of the economy.[78]

Of course, this is the part you were supposed to forget by now, lest the technocrats who want to keep you as their locked-up serfs have their agenda compromised...

Trump personally switched tunes on whether governors would be able to determine the time to do this for their own states[79] or whether federal mandates would be imposed in order to bring about his policy.[80]

---

[76] Ibid.

[77] United States, White House, Executive. (2020, March 16). *15 Days to Slow the Spread*. Retrieved December 16, 2020, from: https://www.whitehouse.gov/articles/15-days-slow-spread/

[78] Liptak, K., Vazquez, M., & Acosta, N. J. (2020, March 25). *Trump says he wants the country 'opened up and just raring to go by Easter', despite health experts' warnings*. CNN. Retrieved December 16, 2020, from https://edition.cnn.com/2020/03/24/politics/trump-easter-economy-coronavirus/index.html

[79] *Trump completes reversal, telling govs 'you are going to call your own shots' and distributes new guidelines*. (2020, April 16). CNN. Retrieved December 16, 2020, from: https://www.cnn.com/2020/04/16/politics/donald-trump-reopening-guidelines-coronavirus/index.html

[80] Blake, A. (2020, April 13). *Trump's propaganda-laden, off-the-rails*

In this way, he already compromised his political messaging on whether or not he preferred 9th and 10th Amendment deference to local authorities or the federal strongman imposing his policies as he wishes. A minor crack in the image but still, a notable one. This initial aim was kept to with varying degrees of success. There was certainly an effort across high levels of government to reopen the economy, the original Coronavirus Task Force headed up by Vice President Mike Pence turned its auspices towards the task in May.[81]

This stood in stark contrast to what much of the other organs of government were doing during the same time.

It was stated in the previous section that the Trump administration's torching of the economy was bad enough without other occurrences.

Then Lafayette Square happened.

In quite possibly one of the most tasteless photo ops in recent memory, riot control tactics and tear gas[82] (meant broadly, rather than the specific CS tear gas formulation not used on that day, before the MAGA clan jump in the air with their 'gotcha's!',

coronavirus briefing. The Washington Post. Retrieved December 16, 2020, from:
https://www.washingtonpost.com/politics/2020/04/13/trumps-propaganda-laden-off-the-rails-coronavirus-briefing/

[81] Liptak, K. (2020, May 6). *In reversal, Trump says task force will continue 'indefinitely'—eyes vaccine czar*. CNN. Retrieved December 16, 2020, from:
https://edition.cnn.com/2020/05/06/politics/trump-task-force-vaccine/index.html

[82] Zhao, C. (2021). *Tear Gas Used on Protesters Near Donald Trump's Church Photo Op*, D.C. Police Attorney Admits. Newsweek. Retrieved 4 June 2021, from:
https://www.newsweek.com/tear-gas-used-protesters-near-donald-trumps-church-photo-op-dc-police-attorney-admits-1596245.

provided by silver tongued lawyers) were deployed by law enforcement officers from the famous square and its surrounding streets, to clear them of protestors who, all records show had been peaceful in D.C., more than can be said for other cities in the country...So the President and the last few sycophants standing could take a stroll across gas swept streets and pose for a photo in front of a church, whilst holding a Bible...upside down...and talk about how he was the President of 'law and order.' 'He who must say "I am the King" is no true King.'

I submit that a President who must bring law and order at the barrels of a glorified occupation force is a President who has misunderstood both.

But before moving onto this point, one objection must be handled—the recent report stating that the actions taken at Lafayette Square did not occur so that the photo op may occur, but were simply a coincidence. No matter how true this may be, and no matter how underreported some will argue it is given other arguments out there to the contrary, its publication after the fact matters little for Trump's image, but especially during his Presidency. Assuming he does not secure another, it may fade into a footnote of history. It should still be noted that the choice to seemingly capitalise on the clearing of Lafayette, even if unintentional, should have been obvious to White House spin doctors.

Back to the previous point, which is to say that it has always seemed a paradoxical outlook that Presidents think they can establish a strong record on law and order by tyrannising protestors, or seeming to, in times of public outcry.

Think Kent State University and its Vietnam War protest for a microcosmic example and one which was far more severe than Lafayette.

Similarly, if police don't want to be treated as occupiers, maybe they shouldn't bastardise the national flag in question, ala

Thin Blue Line.

Certainly, one may argue deterrence has a role in criminal justice and lowering crime rates, though it seems to depend more on publicity of the punishment and less its severity, as people often forget, and more still simply do not know. It is worth adding that even this is contested and is one of the safer technical assertions about the value of deterrence—despite what movies may portray, the value of such policies is far from proven.

It is also true that a feeling of security is key to investor confidence and as such the economic success as a community, see the revitalisation of Chicago.

Though traditional conservatives will often jump the gun here and equate a feeling of security (whilst, lacking reflection, they criticise their opponents for desiring precisely what they brand police as selling) with state police presence, unfairly pre-empting the libertarian argument for privatised security and arbitration by playing definition-fu.

But the idea that brutalising people already disregarding the law, where that disregard is itself downstream of a focal instance where the law was actually or perceived to have been disregarded by any party, which of the two occurred and which party breached the law on the view in question matters little at this stage, such approaches seem to me little more than bloodlust masquerading as a desire for order.

Perhaps that's unfair, a desire for order may still be present, but even the rudimentary examination above shows the logical illiteracy of such a policy. A success in law and order would be, by every sensible estimate, one where these circumstances had never existed to begin with. This does not mean or call for the abolition of the police without a privatised alternative to provide security, as the dystopian leftists have cried louder and louder throughout 2020 and beyond, with predictable results.

All I seek to argue is that, the perspective created when the traditional conservative sees the leftist mobilising violence to infringe his rights, is probably vice versa when that traditional conservative glorifies the bloodshed of his own countrymen he supposedly loves as 'law and order.'

This may be up for consideration when they come to proselytise in the run up to 2024.

Content to pour fuel on the fire, Trump used this opportunity to threaten governors: they would deploy their own National Guards or he would deploy the US Military for them, on their own soil, and: 'quickly solve the problem.'

The 9th Amendment always has been underused in the libertarian view in yet another constitutional tragedy—from here on we may safely say that it has been outright forgotten.

Speaking of the law and lawsuits, many actions were subsequently filed under 1st Amendment freedom of assembly concerning the actions themselves taken at Lafayette.

Time will tell of their success, though it should not be forgotten that the Roberts Court will be, in my estimation and any elementary analysis of where it has granted *certiorari*, far keener to strike down this element of the Trump legacy than its unconstitutional movement against the Second Amendment.[83]

Presidential Rhetoric and Its Cost

In order to understand how COVID-19 affected the political prospects of Trump, we must focus on his and his administration's communication therein.

Whilst we may not know that falsehoods uttered during this period were lies on Trump's part, we do know that they were just that, false. These included exaggerations of the time taken to

---

[83] *BumpstockCase.com, Bumpstock Lawsuit—Guedes v. BATFE.* (2021, June 10). Firearms Policy Coalition. https://www.firearmspolicy.org/guedes-v-batfe

develop a vaccine, as well as the reactions his government and corporations had taken. Trump also politically hijacked health briefings, using them either to promote his own agenda and actions or criticise others for failures, especially Democrats.

Excessive detail in the line of reference work is not desirable here, but rather let us compare this approach to those of other Presidents who have led through times of crisis. Let's compare first to standalone speeches. First, FDR's election in 1933 in the height of The Great Depression. The famous line followed: 'The only thing we have to fear is fear itself.' [84]

Most people can only cite an adaptation of that line from Hermione Granger in Harry Potter, but its near survival in that form just shy of 80 years after the fact is testament to its simple power. FDR's policies may have been awful.

The way our students all across the Anglosphere are educated about The New Deal may be some of the most flagrantly dishonest teaching on economics there is in our schools. It is undeniable though, that the rhetoric through the radio on the mantlepiece by the fire, quite simply, worked.

There is something to be said in Trump's initial disadvantage compared to opponents with a greater command of the English language. This doesn't necessarily have to involve arcane language or prolixity; for another example from FDR consider the opening to his famous fireside chat in March of the same year: 'My friends.' [85]

A simple, universal phrase to unite troubled Americans,

[84] *Who Said, "We Have Nothing to Fear Except Fear Itself"?* (2020, April 3). Interesting Literature. https://interestingliterature.com/2020/04/nothing-fear-except-fear-itself-quotation-origin/

[85] Harris, W. (2021). *Celebrating the First Fireside Chat.* National Archives. https://fdr.blogs.archives.gov/2021/03/10/celebrating-the-first-fireside-chat/

where Trump's strategy of divide and conquer failed to carry the votes a populace quietly fed up of civil disobedience and tired of being incited to hate their own neighbours. Hate is powerful; it's also exhausting. An elementary survey of early modern French history will confirm this. A far greater political seduction, as the seminal book itself says, would be to speak of grand moral issues[86]—remember: 'when we go high, they go low?' YouTube stars certainly did and furthered the Biden cause, deliberately or not, by adapting it into popular media. If one is going to be divisive, use it to galvanise, rather than merely for the sake of incitation.

In the face of the Challenger space shuttle disaster, President Reagan said that 'we will never forget them nor the last time we saw them...[87]—Trump could easily have done the same in consoling family members. It would have gone a long way to defuse Biden's narrative on family deaths as a result of COVID; one should cast their mind back to the astonishing claim from Biden that: 'If you're missing a relative around your table, it's his fault.'

Yet there was nothing of the kind.

Even closer to what would have been needed is George W. Bush's speech to 'Get On Board' encouraging people to keep spending after 9/11, aiming to retain some sense of normality and keep confidence afloat. The only role as consumer-in-chief Trump seemed to play was that of an amateur golfer. This was, of course, a politically relatable activity to the key lower-middle class voters his campaign depended on swinging to win...

The central point is this: Trump's rhetoric, seeking to divide and conquer, worked well in 2016 when new left-wing elements

---

[86] Greene, R. (2004). *The art of seduction.* Profile.
[87] Garber, S. (2004, June 7). *Reagan's Address to the Nation.* Www.history.nasa.gov.
https://www.history.nasa.gov/reagan12886.html

were first making major public cultural gains by galvanising fearful conservative elements against them and the other candidate who was even less popular than him on reputation.

'Crooked Hilary' was a prerequisite for that strategy to work—she could be made into an icon of those encroaching socialists come to take your rights, and that image may well be truer than many give it credit for, precisely because it was so politically motivated.

By contrast, Joe Biden came along with an air of quiet competence, or at least the ability to project an illusion of that air. No matter the degree to which one thinks the facts reflect that air, doubtless a decreasing number given the events of August 2021, a campaign based on unifying the American people against a regime he painted as incompetent and undeserving, the tool of division became ineffectual.

Hence, we find ourselves here, with Trump trumped and Biden intent on breaking the back of his nation's economy to strengthen the knees of his own legacy.

Government Action Elsewhere

No matter the growth of the American people's finances under the Trump administration, it was difficult for this to manifest without a united Congress in a time of such divided politics. This is because, for those not yet in the know, the House of Representatives, the lower house in the U.S. Congress, is constitutionally mandated as the point of origin for all 'money bills'—all bills involving government spending.

The constitutional intent behind this was to keep the American people's public purse under the primary jurisdiction of their most vulnerable and strongly incentivised representatives (all House seats cycle every two years as opposed to the Presidency every four and Senate every six).

So it was intended that any spurious spending would swiftly result in the Representatives in question being removed; future representatives would be aware of this incentive and modulate their behaviour accordingly.

Oh, if only…

When the House and Presidency are in the hands of opposite parties, it becomes very difficult for the policy of the executive to manifest in fiscal terms where there is divergence between the two. Unusually in this case, the House was aiming to spend more than the President and outshine him in most cases in the run up to the election, rather than shoot down his spending plans and politically hamstring him—see 6 of the 8 Obama years.

Initial spending was outrageous enough—$2.5 trillion across two months of March and April.

Moreover, a second argument can be noted as to the poor Constitutional design at play here. The Founders presumed, seemingly correctly to them if they were exporting their view onto every citizen, though that would in itself be a mistake, that playing deficit hawk with their own elected representatives was firstly possible and secondly a profitable use of the citizenry's time, and that those conditions would continue to be true from thereon out.

It is a sad testament to the current state of affairs that the first proviso must be raised, but raised it must be.

The American education system provides an ironically fitting example here.

Contrary to public perception and instinct in much of the UK and abroad as far as I can tell, wrote whole the U.S. actually spends an exorbitant sum of money in terms of per capita education, one of the highest in the world. Yet it consistently underperforms those who spend less up to a certain margin, never mind those who spend more. Why this is the case could not be done justice here on account of it being such a sociologically complex phenomenon, nor would it be of total relevance to the point being made. The highlights, as far as they prove the point that some plurality of citizens no longer accurately can, and a larger group cannot profitably engage in monitoring their representatives, will do.

CARES From the Uncaring—The Congressional Response

The Coronavirus Aid, Relief, and Economic Security Act (CARES) Act should briefly be covered. This is to cover the exact decisions the Trump administration made and precisely who it betrayed in the process.

The Trump regime signed the $2.4 trillion dollar bill into place for their American subjects on March 27th, 2020.[88] The first $300 billion of spending which it authorised consisted primarily of one time cash payments to Americans on the order of $1,200 with families receiving more.[89] The next $260 billion increased new and pre-existing unemployment benefits.[90] Next came the Paycheck Protection Program which was empowered to grant a total of $350 billion in small business loans which were forgivable on the

[88] Hulse, C. (2020, July 11). *As Coronavirus Spread, Largest Stimulus in History United a Polarized Senate.* The New York Times. Retrieved December 21, 2020, from:
https://www.nytimes.com/2020/03/26/us/coronavirus-senate-stimulus-package.html

[89] Sauter, M. (2020, October 13). *Coronavirus stimulus checks: Here's how many people will get $1,200 in every state.* USA Today. Retrieved December 21, 2020, from:
https://www.usatoday.com/story/money/2020/04/28/how-many-people-will-get-1200-in-every-state/111604090/

[90] Snell, K. (2020, July 11). *What's Inside The Senate's $2 Trillion Coronavirus Aid Package.* NPR. Retrieved December 21, 2020, from https://www.npr.org/2020/03/26/821457551/whats-inside-the-senate-s-2-trillion-coronavirus-aid-package

condition that employers kept the number of employees under them and their wages stable. This was later increased to $669 billion by the Paycheck Protection Program and Health Care Enhancement Act, being signed into law on April 24th alongside other legislation, but that act did the majority of the damage, weighing in at $484 billion.[91] Half a trillion went to loans for corporations and the final remainder, some $339.8 billion to state and local governments.[92]

So, by far the largest single relief package in US history,[93] totalling some 10% of GDP at the time of passing. More than twice the size of the $831 billion package passed in response to The Great Recession.[94] And all in response from lawmakers to a crisis they had at large brought on, at the expense of the American people, as the countervailing examples prove.

It is a deception on their part, aided and abetted in the media, that it was the virus in and of itself which caused these economic

[91] Foran, C. (2021). *House approves $480 billion package to help small businesses and hospitals, expand Covid-19 testing.* CNN. Retrieved 5 June 2021, from: https://edition.cnn.com/2020/04/23/politics/house-vote-small-business-aid-vote/index.html.

[92] Snell, K. (2021). *What's Inside The Senate's $2 Trillion Coronavirus Aid Package.* Text.npr.org. Retrieved 5 June 2021, from https://text.npr.org/821457551.

[93] Cochrane, E., & Stolberg, S. G. (2020, March 27). *$2 Trillion Coronavirus Stimulus Bill Is Signed Into Law.* The New York Times. Retrieved December 21, 2020, from: https://www.nytimes.com/2020/03/27/us/politics/coronavirus-house-voting.html

[94] Kambhampati, S. (2020, March 26). *The coronavirus stimulus package versus the Recovery Act.* The Los Angeles Times. Retrieved December 21, 2020, from: https://www.latimes.com/politics/story/2020-03-26/coronavirus-stimulus-package-versus-recovery-act

malaises which in turn manifest in people's suffering being enhanced many times fold. This is true both in the present and future—children will suffer the burden of adult zeal in destruction of liberty.

It was the ham-fisted response of *zeitgeist* pursuing intelligentsia rejects who threw their own citizens under house arrest which caused this crisis, and they must be held accountable for that action.

The supreme irony is that those who protested on grounds of genuine opposition to this policy, were those who ended up targeted by the willing mouthpieces of the lawmakers.

Don't believe me?

Anti-lockdown protestors were characterised as 'armed militias' based off of a single incident in Michigan by The New York Times,[95] and according to the Guardian, when dealing with those guilty of wrongthink, cellphone data is compelling evidence of risk to public health.[96]

Operation Prism flashbacks anyone?

Studies have already come out showing that protests did not increase infection rates significantly in the case of BLM protestors,[97] so why any different for those expressing

---

[95] Associated Press. (2020, May 2). *Michigan Militia Puts Armed Protest in the Spotlight*. The New York Times. Retrieved December 21, 2020, from:
https://web.archive.org/web/20200505023314/https://www.nytimes.com/aponline/2020/05/02/us/politics/ap-us-outbreak-protests.html

[96] Wilson, J. (2020, May 18). *US lockdown protests may have spread virus widely, cellphone data suggests*. The Guardian. Retrieved December 21, 2020, from:
https://www.theguardian.com/us-news/2020/may/18/lockdown-protests-spread-coronavirus-cellphone-data

[97] Beer, T. (2020, July 1). *Research Determines Protests Did Not Cause*

disagreement with this policy, at least as far as transmission rates only are concerned?

Forgive the lawyer in me for asking questions with obvious conclusions; because those protesting the lockdown policy directly were never going to vote Biden and so were fair targets for his ersatz media militants. Heaven forbid the same companies and agenda-driven outlets, motivated by profit as much as anyone else, even ask the same questions of other protestors whose cause was found to be more marketable, courtesy again of their good friend the *zeitgeist*.

The first warning alarm for specific instances of the economy outside of modelling was the airline industry. As early as March, predictions were made that no airlines would survive the global closing of borders without immediate government assistance and in mid-March, a conglomerate group of airlines in the US requested $50 billion in a federal bailout.[98] Next came restaurants, requesting a further $145 billion.[99]

Perhaps fearing some semblance of fiscal responsibility remaining in the Senate, Steve Mnuchin, Secretary of the Treasury, told Senate Republicans that unemployment could reach as high as

---

Spike In Coronavirus Cases. Forbes. Retrieved December 21, 2020, from:

https://www.forbes.com/sites/tommybeer/2020/07/01/research-determines-protests-did-not-cause-spike-in-coronavirus-cases/

[98] Buncombe, A. (2021). Coronavirus: *US airline industry asks for $50bn in government bailout to counter drop in demand.* The Independent. Retrieved 5 June 2021, from:

https://www.independent.co.uk/news/world/americas/coronavirus-us-airlines-funding-flights-emergency-funding-a9405031.html.

[99] Lucas, A. (2021). *Restaurant industry asks for $145 billion recovery fund from the government.* CNBC. Retrieved 5 June 2021, from https://www.cnbc.com/2020/03/18/restaurant-industry-asks-for-145-billion-recovery-fund-from-the-government.html.

20% if nothing was done and that 3.3 million Americans had filed for unemployment in one week ending March 21st. This would be multiple times the previous record set in 1982 of 695,000.[100]

Investment banks produced hugely variable predictions on GDP decline for the second quarter of 2020; Deustche Bank predicted 12.9% shrinkage[101] against Goldman Sachs' 24%: 'in response to the Coronavirus pandemic.[102]

We've already discussed how that's a half-truth so significant it should be counted as a lie at this stage. The shrinkage was not in response to the pandemic, it was in response to the government's handling of the pandemic.

The linguistic point again bears reiteration here—unemployment would not have had any potential to soar to 20% if the government had not taken the actions that it did, and the huge shrinkages were not due to the pandemic itself.

---

[100] Hussain, S. (2021). *Coronavirus: Record number of Americans file for unemployment*. BBC News. Retrieved 5 June 2021, from https://www.bbc.co.uk/news/business-52050426.

[101] Winck, B. (2021). *The worst global recession since World War II: Deutsche Bank just unveiled a bleak new forecast as the coronavirus rocks economies worldwide*. Markets Insider. Retrieved 5 June 2021, from:https://markets.businessinsider.com/news/stocks/coronavirus-recession-worst-wwii-economic-recovery-global-deutsche-bank-2020-3-1029012757?utm_source=msn.com&utm_medium=referral&utm_content=msn-slideshow&utm_campaign=bodyurl.

[102] Reinicke, C. (2021). *Goldman Sachs now says US GDP will shrink 24% next quarter amid the coronavirus pandemic—which would be 2.5 times bigger than any decline in history*. Markets Insider. Retrieved 5 June 2021, from: https://markets.businessinsider.com/news/stocks/us-gdp-drop-record-2q-amid-coronavirus-recession-goldman-sachs-2020-3-1029018308?utm_source=msn.com&utm_medium=referral&utm_content=msn-slideshow&utm_campaign=bodyurl.

George Beglan

Both were symptomatic of the Trump administration's response, not the virus itself.

It seems, in yet another irony, that the cure of the Trump regime was far worse than the disease, words he used to ward off concerns about the intensity of his intervention. He may have attempted to use his signature on the income bills distributed pursuant to the Act to show a caring side prior to the election, but, should the author have anything to say about it, that signature will here be remembered for the irresponsibility of his government in betraying the very principles of liberty of the nation it was supposedly leading and to which it should accordingly have been beholden.

Mitch McConnell was one of the first to publicly acknowledge seeing the dangers of further increased spending, and so, initially, warned against any more. The Democrat-controlled house attempted to pass a further $3 trillion under the proposed HEROES Act in May on a vote of 208-199. The bill, thank the heavens, was marked as 'dead on arrival' in the Senate and as such did not pass, though there may be successive attempts.

After this significant defeat, both parties engaged in a deadlock of proposing spending bills along the lines of their own special interests, with each hypocritically criticising the other on the charge of including them. There were already enough of them in the CARES Act such as the Ashford Hospitality Trust, amongst others. Almost like Washington's warnings about a two-party system ring truer and truer each passing year, no?

However, this was not to stay. The lame-duck session brought with it new uncertainty for policy after the handover to Biden. So the Senate came to bipartisan agreement on further spending; a plan for some further $908 billion presented on December 14th and variants discussed before an agreement on one come the 19th.

More followed in 2021 but be patient dear reader, we'll get

to that red meat soon enough.

American Jurisprudence under COVID-19—Infected with a Corollary Plague

We have already touched on this subject briefly but it bears expansion here. I have already aligned myself with the admittedly heterodox view that *Marbury v Madison* is completely unjustified. It takes the Supreme Court outside the bounds of its power per any strict reading of the Constitution and no Federalist Paper seems to, on my reading, indicate that it should be given the power which the case affords it.

Scholarly opinion during the pandemic seems to have run to the contrary direction, disturbingly so.

One Cambridge Law Journal article which would come up towards the top of most search engines if one was to enter the first half of this section's title concerns a hypothesis of just the opposite—what the authors term 'executive underreach' during the pandemic.

The very demands such an idea would make in its practical deployment seem dangerously irreconcilable with tradition of Anglospheric administrative law—such a doctrine would have to underpinned by the idea that courts could compel the other branches into action on account of an omission and nothing else.

That is to say, not just an omission pursuant to another legally valent action; a failure to compensate for seized or purchased property under the 5th Amendment in the U.S. for example.

But that a court could compel a legislative, executive, or other administrative body into action as the first action in the concerned series of events carrying positive legal valence. The parallel evolution of judicial activism (at least the explicit kind) in the U.S. far beyond the UK, both underpinned and masked by the faux approach of 'loose constructivism' makes the U.S. a far more attractive jurisdiction in which to mount such an argument, at least semantically.

It would be unfair to omit that the scholars correctly point out themselves that there would be numerous roadblocks against such a thing becoming part of U.S. law in actuality, thank the heavens.

But it is also an essential component of judicial neutrality that this not be the case; that courts be institutions of review, rather than proactive alignment. One can make this point out on many familiar grounds—some would restate the unelected nature of the judiciary and its according place outside representation.

I prefer the point that this approach is also an open invitation for judges to enforce their own policy as and where the opportunity presents itself.

Failing even that, their biases may shine through in the judgments they make and the cases they decide to hear; we already see the dangers of this with the selective granting of *certiorari* in the U.S. as the circumstances are constituted.

The Divided States of America

One might think the above title a worn out phrase; I beg to differ. Gone may be the days where the majority of Americans felt more loyalty to state than the federal royalty, but variance in the attitude of states at their own level to managing COVID-19 has been a subject of much comment.

There has been varying intent within that comment—much is political point scoring but some good scientific discussion can also follow on the variation between states policies. There has been variability within states as counties have come up with varying responses, but states can broadly be grouped by: the presence or not of stay at home orders, the requirement or not of face coverings in public, what degree of restrictions were put into place on gatherings, restrictions on travelling between states and the closures of businesses ordered. It is worth stating at the outset that no state took a completely voluntarist outlook and all struck down the liberty of their constituents to some degree.

Disappointing?

Yes, but at least, predictably and consistently so.

The only major areas of concern to declare a state of emergency outside of the month of March were the North Marianas, in January and Washington State, in February.

Stay at home orders (the vast majority of which were lifted in April or May, only a few in June) were put into place in all areas except the American Samoa, Arkansas, Guam, Iowa, Nebraska, North Dakota, and the North Marianas. They were declared unconstitutional in Wisconsin after 6-7 weeks whilst some states only had regional or partial orders, these being Wyoming, Utah, Oklahoma, Massachusetts, South Dakota and Kentucky.

Examining these states by the party of the Governors therein yields interesting results.

Four Democrats, eleven Republicans.

More Democrats than one might think, whilst still the minority, though this is predictable. This trend becomes especially true when expanding the analysis to the considerably greater number of states which did not demand facial coverings be worn outside. It is regrettable that the issue of liberty is so often turned into a partisan one, but governors responsible directly to their constituents showing in their partisan alignment at least a contested field shows some promise; it's not all Republicans protecting liberty.

By the same token, it's not all Democrats infringing on liberty.

Some Republican governors took actions within their states which strongly infringed that liberty. Moreover, this is the stage where we can begin to leave the Trump reaction to COVID behind and begin to examine the Biden continuation. It definitely hit the ground running, with a federal mask mandate on the first day of its administration.

Again, what 9th and 10th Amendment? It took another day for Biden to further carve his nation apart and immediately undo any unifying process of his own campaign by turning a biological issue into a racial issue, signing an executive order mentioning the idea of systemic racism when setting up a new testing regime.

It took still scant little time more for Biden to decide that he wanted to take one of the most consistently well-performing measures for a first-term President—start a war. Only, his position and circumstances didn't allow for any immediate expedition into the Middle East, so to war with COVID-19 it was.

He claimed that the 400,000 total domestic deaths at the time was greater than all American deaths in WWI, WWII and Vietnam combined[103]—not technically true, though loyal Biden media lapdogs wouldn't tell you that.

We priorly established just how outrageous CARES was a solution to the economic issues at hand.

Biden, though defeated by teleprompters and staircases, was not to be outdone in just how many dollars he could print.

So came the American Rescue Plan Act of 2021. A further $1.9 trillion. Remember the previous section where I made the point that the House has to be the origin of all money bills? Democrats didn't—attempting to sneak a $15 per hour minimum wage into the last stages of a Senate debate on recovery stimulus for a pandemic, only for it to be struck out in reconciliatory stages

---

[103] AP FACT CHECK: *Biden on virus deaths, Kerry's climate crisis.* (2021, February 25). The Independent. https://www.independent.co.uk/news/world/americas/us-politics/ap-fact-check-biden-on-virus-deaths-kerrys-climate-crisis-joe-biden-ap-john-kerry-americans-vietnam-b1807041.html

of debate on the bill, is thematic of the Biden administration so far.

Use the easy applause lights in public because we've got nothing else to say and sneak anything in controversial in through the backdoor. I don't mean to deviate too far into unrelated criticism of the Biden regime more broadly, despite its controversial management of the interior and other subjects. However, as before, the point still stands that this recession seems almost entirely government manufactured, at least in its immediate severity. The yield curve may have been indicative that a correction was necessary, but not on the order of printing just shy of another $2 trillion dollars after 35% of all dollars in circulation by the end of 2020 were printed in that year.[104]

One might say that far worse in the longer run than wipeable and recoverable sums of money was the open embrace of authoritarian tactics by the Biden administration. Concerns were already raised about running mate Kamala Harris, courtesy of Tulsi Gabbard.

For those in need of a reminder, charges include being more than willing to throw the people she supposedly most cared about in cages whilst laughing on national media about the same charge she'd used to cage them during her time as a prosecutor and knowingly withholding evidence that would have gotten prisoners off of death row.[105]

There, in short, were early warning signs of the very same

[104] Choros, J. (2020, December 16). *35% of All U.S. Dollars in Existence Have Been Printed in the Last 10 Months.* Netcoins. https://netcoins.ca/blog/35-of-all-u-s-dollars-in-existence-have-been-printed-last-in-10-months/?__cf_chl_jschl_tk__=pmd_c67bfc71b4c94248ffec4ba16c4f1ec18c7dd47f-1629221103-0-gqNtZGzNAnijcnBszQii

[105] CNN. (2019). *Tulsi Gabbard rips Kamala Harris' record on criminal prosecutions* [YouTube Video]. In *YouTube.* https://www.youtube.com/watch?v=Y4fjA0K2EeE

tactics they decried the Trump administration using in their own behaviour, to the surprise of nobody paying attention.

At 12.50 AM on May 14th of 2021, Joe Biden decided that he'd hid his power-hungry tendencies well enough to sneak into an unassailable position and tweeted out the following:

> *The rule is now simple: get vaccinated or wear a mask until you do. The choice is yours.*[106]

That is no longer just a ninth or tenth Amendment issue, that's now about bodily autonomy and integrity.

Specifically, either accepting that the state had the right to violate that integrity at will, or impose a condition upon you until you acquiesced to such a violation—the state can, on Biden's view, give itself the right to coerce consent from its subjects.

If a private individual attempted this, they would rightfully be convicted of a heinous felony.

When the state does it, it's virtuous, on his view. Again, I do not deny the effectiveness or desirability of vaccines, but again, on my view for a right to be human it must be derived from one's own humanity and thereby only assailable by a vector which I presume nobody sane wishes to engage in, denial of that humanity.

Margins of appreciation and other ersatz ways in which the state has inserted itself into places it has no right to can be damned, either rights are human or they are not. There does not seem a more inherent one than the right to one's own body, if one accepts the view that the human status and condition conveys rights in the first place, seeing as nothing about that humanity is

[106] DeMarche, E. (2021, May 14). *Biden's COVID-19 "rule" tweet panned on social media.* Fox News. https://www.foxnews.com/politics/bidens-covid-19-rule-tweet-panned-on-social-media

more immediately obvious than your own body.

But the Biden administration, alongside the EU precedent priorly discussed, seems to be attempting to transform human rights into what I suggest we call: 'normal rights'—rights present in times of normalcy but subject to removal, edition and suspension by the government at will.

Some of you may clamour that this will only happen in times of crisis but recall the prior point on incentive. Once you make a power subject to a criterion, Goodhart's law applies and governments will find a way to force given circumstances into that criterion, including by outright editing the definition of that criterion where they can get away with it.

You will also remember that this is exactly the opposite of the original intention behind the chief development of human rights law after WWII; to limit governments and hold them accountable. Such an inversion is a statement to how far liberty has fallen and how direly the communities of the world have abandoned their vigilance of that liberty.

Some reference to and discussion of *mens rea* is necessary for both nuance and accuracy. It is almost certainly the case, at least I hope, that those enacting and supporting the policies in question do not conceptualise them this way or create some doctrine of exception and self-exemption to discharge the moral load that, I also hope, would otherwise be overwhelming.

So it is that we should not treat our fellow person and common supporter of these policies in the same way we would treat individuals who knowingly and actively disregard the consent of others. They can hardly be blamed in a 'cradle-to-grave' or as I think it is better put 'stable-to-abattoir' education and social management system designed to churn out tax cattle to fuel the glorified statist Ponzi schemes and nought else.

A culture which openly embraces authoritarianism to the point of decrying critical thinking as an idea predictably creates such individuals. We must not treat them as enemies at first encounter then, but attempt to snap them out of the state induced delusion they live in.

After all, though voluntarism is the natural state of play at birth if it is a natural ethic, and it would follow that the burden of proof would actually lie on the statists to prove their benefits, this logical redoubt does not reflect the situation as the people we must convert think of it.

Moreover, as goes the culture, so goes the law, given enough time and sufficient force of will. Given legal systems may impose stronger and stronger redoubts against the fickle and fading throes of a mob, such as is done in the U.S., but no safeguard is ever total.

My chief concern moving forward is that this response to COVID-19, authoritarian on both sides of the 'aisle' marks the shift towards a greater tolerance of such approaches in the country, and in the rest of the world as following its lead. Indeed, the reversion of the Biden Presidency to Trump policies which the Biden Campaign objected so strongly to, surely puts lie to the idea that there is even a political aisle in the U.S.

For examples in the last few years of the fact that there is no aisle, just statists in different colour ties, see border camps (which Kamala took until June to visit,[107] and even then only under significant public pressure), police militarisation[108] and drug policy, which was pointed out during the campaign.

You might also compare Biden's rant at one unlucky CNN

---

[107] *Vice-President Kamala Harris to make first trip to border.* (2021, June 24). BBC News. https://www.bbc.co.uk/news/world-us-canada-57589360
[108] Semler, S. (2021, April 4). *The Flow Of Military Equipment To Police Has Accelerated Under Biden.* PopularResistance.org. https://popularresistance.org/the-flow-of-military-equipment-to-police-has-accelerated-under-biden/

reporter,[109] and the network's prompt throwing of that reporter under the bus in order to maintain good graces with their emperor, a different image than that of Trump's often mentioned spat with Fox News.

The more reflective amongst our ranks may have recently had the disturbing thought that our opponents may hold a compelling utilitarian argument—if people are willing to tolerate this authoritarianism, no matter how disgusting we find it and there is some provable advantage to policy in its use, what leg do we have to stand on?

I also mention this as a pre-emption of this argument likely being used by the very same authoritarians. The immediate responses are twofold: firstly, that there may not be any provable advantage, see Sweden and Switzerland. Secondly that as far as deontology still applies, this argument is limited, and it's difficult for authoritarians within the Overton Window to make a case for unlimited utilitarianism these days, thanks to WWII and the Marxist inspired governments around the world which followed with atrocities innumerable.

So it is from this terrifying thought that we must drive our clamour.

Where corporatist platforms move to censor free speech, create alternatives. Where providers conspire to de-platform those alternatives, file antitrust actions in jurisdictions with strong records for punitive and/or exemplary damages.

Wherever a government would seek to make you dependent, become the exact opposite.

---

[109] Johnson, B. (2021, June 16). *WATCH: Biden Screams At CNN Reporter Who Questioned Him: "You're In The Wrong Business."* The Daily Wire. https://www.dailywire.com/news/watch-biden-screams-at-cnn-reporter-who-questioned-him-youre-in-the-wrong-business

Operations like the Free State Project and Seasteading have been making great strides in this arena but are insufficient to achieve critical mass on their own. I genuinely believe and hold that, if we tame our more cynical tendencies to laugh at the political process (and make no mistake, it is laughable, but it is the laughable catastrophe currently holding a monopoly on violence we are presented with nonetheless.) we have the arguments necessary to defeat our opponents.

Some may point to President Biden's obvious mental decline and people's tolerance of it as an indication that statism has never been stronger. That may be true, but there is a contrary submission, and failing that a dismissal. The contrary submission is to look first of all to the average age of Presidential candidates from 2016 onwards. Significantly above average, especially if one weights for popularity of the candidates throughout the process, rather than taking a crude mean average of age across the field.

What's the significance?

First of all, it's a reversion of the simple economic expectation.

If anything, one would expect a younger field based on the lowered barriers to entry the internet would bring about; younger candidates would be better able to enter, so would and the average age would accordingly drop. Yet this seems to be an America calling out for some semblance of familiarity to compartmentalise the destruction of the public trust away. An America so blinded by the spotlights of its vaunted few that it has lost the ability to turn away, see the half-serious discussion of Obama 3 in 2016, which would require repealing a constitutional amendment.

Combine this with the fact that trust in the government is at an all time low amongst young and upcoming voters (the label sickens me, young people could aspire to be millions of greater things, but discuss it we must) and you have a fertile ground for libertarians and voluntarists to make ground against statists who have dominated since Hoover.

The show must go on, and old age must eventually take those who have dominated up until now. As and when this happens, I predict a disorientation.

It will be an Obama 2016 problem on steroids—he had dominated the party image so thoroughly that there was no clear successor when he uttered those iconic words 'Obama Out.'

In the next 10 years, with the likely loss of multiple household names, we may see the same phenomenon across the entirety of the U.S. cultural and political landscape.

It will be in that disorientation that we must fight our blitzkrieg for whatever precious little is left of Columbia's soul.

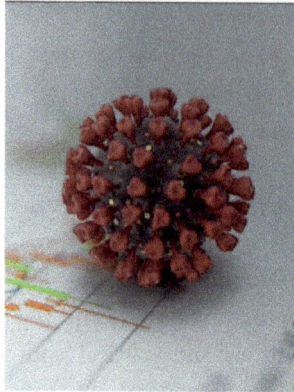

Chapter 5—COVID-1984 in the UK, a Nation of Hypocrites Obsessed with Image

Liberty does not exist in the absence of morality.
—Edmund Burke

The Johnson Hypocrisy—Project Fear

THE TITLE OF this section is an intentional reference.

Those of you who followed the Brexit referendum and surrounding campaigns some years prior may remember the characterisation of the 'remain' campaign as 'Project Fear', most notably by Boris Johnson, long before he was Prime Minister, but first in the 2014 referendum on Scottish independence.[110]

The greatest irony however, is that, if one was to summate the First Johnson Ministry in two words, his own 'Project Fear' would be an excellent choice, on account of the open psychological warfare he has waged on his own people,[111] which should in and of itself be enough for de-election, if not outright prosecution.

We must be fair in our criticism. Many thought that, after the UK's departure from the EU, its handling of the virus would be resoundingly disastrous by comparison. At the first stage of response, lockdown worshippers would clamour that their suspicions were confirmed; the UK was slower to lockdown than its peers and it is arguable that a higher death rate may have followed.[112]

However, this readout could be challenged on the basis of the second half of the response where the UK was a global leader in vaccine rollout,[113] the most successful in the history of the nation, and the seemingly ominous statistical readouts at home can be

---

[110] Gordon, T. (2014, December 21). *I admit it, I'm the man who coined the Project Fear Label.* The Herald. Retrieved March 25, 2021, from: https://www.heraldscotland.com/news/13194407.i-admit-it-the-man-who-coined-project-fear-label/

[111] Rayner, G. (2021, April 2). *State of fear: how ministers "used covert tactics" to keep scared public at home.* The Telegraph. https://www.telegraph.co.uk/news/2021/04/02/state-fear-ministers-used-covert-tactics-keep-scared-public/

[112] Triggle, N. (2020, June 7). *Coronavirus: Lockdown delay 'cost a lot of lives', says science adviser* [BBC discussion of UK lockdown delay]. Retrieved March 25, 2021, from: https://www.bbc.co.uk/news/uk-politics-52955034

[113] Gregory, A. (2021, January 30). *WHO urges UK to pause Covid vaccinations after vulnerable protected to boost global rollout.* The Independent. https://www.independent.co.uk/news/uk/home-news/coronavirus-vaccine-uk-who-eu-b1795125.html

attributed and dispelled across and amongst multiple causes rather than solely blamed on the tardiness to lockdown as discussed previously.

Aside from however the policies of the Johnson Ministry played out amongst the nation, one thing cannot be disputed. The pandemic laid utterly bare the internal hypocrisy of the Ministry from top to bottom, replete with examples, though the same may also be said of other British institutions. From the very start, Johnson either intentionally or by his own negligence, made reference to supposed regulations that did not exist in the laws his own ministry had passed.[114]

What this hypocrisy means may be the more profound and disturbing observation, but it is better discussed at length later. Dominic Cummings and his 'family trip' some 180 miles to County Durham whilst his government was content to extort its citizenry for far lesser journeys may leap to mind.

The contrast of underpolicing of the Black Lives Matter protests,[115] virtuously intended as both parties may have been, against the downright predatory behaviour of some other police forces in other points in time comes to mind. Such behaviours include the stalking of walkers in the Lake District[116] and

[114] Dodd, V., & O'Carroll, L. (2020, March 30). *UK police warned against "overreach" in use of virus lockdown powers.* The Guardian. https://www.theguardian.com/uk-news/2020/mar/30/uk-police-guidelines-coronavirus-lockdown-enforcement-powers-following-criticism-lord-sumption

[115] Dearden, L. (2020, July 22). *Police officers took the knee as they felt pressured to, says Met chief.* The Independent. https://www.independent.co.uk/news/uk/home-news/met-police-blm-take-knee-cressida-dick-a9631811.html

[116] Christodoulou, H. (2020, March 29). *Coronavirus cops who stalked walkers with drones fill blue lagoon with black dye to stop Brits visiting during lockdown.* The Sun. Retrieved March 25, 2021, from

pressuring Parliament to denigrate the rights of protestors,[117] they continue the theme of UK police seeming at least to the public, glorified schoolyard bullies unwilling to take on genuine threats for fear of their own image.

Presumably, the authoritarians reading will reply that it's a case of 'damned if they do, damned if they don't' as shown by the vitriol in the reaction to police treatment of the recent Sarah Everard protestors and the subsequent anti-police sentiment as a result that case.[118]

In the same breath, the NHS has been elevated higher than ever in the esteem of the nation, by the combination of the virtue signalling 'Clap for Carers' scheme,[119] the simple focus on the institution generated by the circumstances, and the opportunities to further entrench the institution presented by said circumstances, taken by every statist in the nation worth their salt.

We will begin however, as the title of the section suggests, with the hypocrisies present in the current government, which the pandemic laid bare.

---

https://www.thesun.co.uk/news/11278109/cornavirus-cops-lagoon-peak-district-lockdown/

[117] *Police, Crime, Sentencing and Courts Bill 2021: protest powers factsheet.* (2021, July 7). GOV.UK. https://www.gov.uk/government/publications/police-crime-sentencing-and-courts-bill-2021-factsheets/police-crime-sentencing-and-courts-bill-2021-protest-powers-factsheet#common-misconceptions

[118] Sarah Everard: *Met Police chief will not resign over vigil scenes.* (2021, March 14). BBC News. https://www.bbc.co.uk/news/uk-56389824

[119] Staff, T. L. B. (2021, January 6). *"Clap For NHS" Virtue Signal to Return to UK [Video] | The Liberty Beacon.* Www.thelibertybeacon.com. https://www.thelibertybeacon.com/clap-for-nhs-virtue-signal-to-return-to-uk-video/

The First Johnson Ministry began imposing lockdowns on March 23 2020. The initial goal which was often touted was to 'flatten the curve',[120] referring to the curves of graphs of viral transmission rates.

The idea was that by slowing down the rate of viral infection and reproduction, one could better protect the public. One might think of this in economic terms as cost restructuring—keep this metaphor in your head as you read this chapter.

That is to say, the Johnson government elected to, instead of paying the cost of COVID upfront, dispel the lump sum over multiple instalments. The huge sums (the metaphorical interest) added to this bill's total by lockdown's trampling on basic human rights, institutionalisation of discrimination in the labour market and eye-watering additional sums of money added to the national debt, ultimately to be forcibly paid off by people existing in the future who could not consent to having such a burden thrust upon them, as discussed in the first chapter, wouldn't matter in the minds of the Johnson ministry, as long as these things weren't in the minds of the electorate come the next election.

Every politically responsible person in the UK must therefore make sure that these are exactly the things on the mind of the electorate come that time.

The first lockdown lasted in one form or another until September, by which time most activities had returned to some sense of normality.

It was not long before cases spiked again, as was an entirely predictable consequence of taking the nation off lockdown before immunity was reached one way or the other: one can restructure

---

[120] Street-Porter, J. (2020, July 30). *When did the policy of "flattening the curve" ruin our lives?* Mail Online. https://www.dailymail.co.uk/news/article-8576889/When-did-policy-flattening-curve-ruin-lives.html

the costs of a transaction across time but it is substantially more difficult to reduce that total cost as a sum.

If the intensity of payments on that cost are directly related to the liberties of the population, or are at least inversely related to the removal of those liberties, then restoring said liberties would cause a spike, as anyone with an IQ greater than 70 would have known ahead of time.

This surge is the much-euphemised 'second wave' and the linguistic trend followed 'third waves', 'fourth waves' and so on. What should be purely descriptive terms have been used to shame anyone who refused to cow to the Johnson Ministry's institutionalisation of fear and stand their ground on the very freedoms the UK first incepted on the political level.

We could have held our ground at this point.

We could have demanded that Parliament lay down its emergency powers, enact the sunset clause on the tyrannical Coronavirus Act and be done with it.

But no, a second lockdown was demanded by the authoritarian and cowardly (I apologise for the tautology, those two groups seem to intersect perfectly) elements of the populace, media and intelligentsia.

One will immediately notice the indecisiveness of this approach compared to the Swedish strategy discussed earlier.

Did it stop there; were the tyrants appeased once we gave them the latest thing they wanted?

Predictably, not.

Tiered restrictions across England and a month-long 'circuit breaker' lockdown began in October, with these tiers revised continually until being abandoned in favour of a third national lockdown shortly after Christmas. This was to be by far the longest, with plans for it to extend in some way or another into the summer of 2021 and towards its Autumn.

The repealing of these steps is supposedly 'irreversible', but seeing as this is the Johnson Ministry we are discussing, I'll believe it when I see it. Two walkbacks have already taken place in regards to the summer lifting by the time of publication, that people will be 'expected' to wear face coverings in public places instead of the matter being one of personal choice, and that the so-called 'Freedom Day' will be July 19th instead of June 21st.

Now that you have the factual background, we can discuss the disastrous mismanagement and hypocrisy of the Johnson Ministry and wider government apparatus in greater detail.

Standing out as hypocrite *primus inter pares* is not the man supposed to hold the Latin title himself, but rather his former hand, one Dominic Cummings, with Matt Hancock coming in close second.

The Prime Minister announced his diagnosis of COVID-19 some 4 days into the first lockdown.

The same day, Cummings received a phone call from his wife in which she described illness and thought she had contracted COVID-19; he rushed home and then took her and his extended family to County Durham in the North of England, supposedly on the justification that his own parents would be able to look after their son should both he and his wife become ill.[121]

The family returned around mid-April, some two weeks after an official government report described Cummings as experiencing COVID-19 symptoms and 'self-isolating at home.'

This report failed to mention the impromptu family trip in blatant violation of lockdown rules, hence the scandal.

Cummings' later explanation attempted to claim that 'there was no regulation to cover the situation he was in'—the police

---

[121] *Dominic Cummings' Durham trip: Timeline of events as minister resigns.* (2020, May 26). ITV News.
https://www.itv.com/news/2020-05-26/dominic-cummings-durham-trip-timeline

later ambivalently said that no offence had been committed in Cummings first journey to Durham and only a minor violation of lockdown restrictions in a small diversion on the return journey via a place called Barnard Castle.[122]

This trend of police taking downright predatory action against those without capacity to defend themselves, whilst letting the powerful get away with violating lockdown ad infinitum, will become a common one.

This was after Cummings had already all but driven out former Chancellor Sajid Javid, who refused to have his aides purged and replaced by Cummings' drones in a cabinet shake-up and resigned accordingly.

All this only for Javid to later return as Health Secretary.

The following media storm tanked confidence in the government; the sector ranked 'most sceptical' quadrupled in 6 months and included 25% of all respondents at the time, according to University College London.[123]

It took until the 14th of November for anything approximating a resignation from Cummings, despite repeated calls for said resignation. Not content with damage done, Cummings then proceeded to release a series of documents further undermining and showing the disunity of the Johnson Ministry.

The Cummings scandal undermined the Johnson Ministry's lockdowns as policy and its wider credibility from the start.

This was followed by other rule-breakers elsewhere in

[122] *Read in full: Durham police statement on Dominic Cummings.* (2020, May 28). Politics Home.
https://www.politicshome.com/news/article/read-in-full-durham-police-statement-on-dominic-cummings
[123] Stone, J. (2020, October 8). *Public trust in UK government coronavirus response sinking, study finds.* The Independent.
https://www.independent.co.uk/news/uk/politics/coronavirus-uk-government-response-boris-johnson-dominic-cummings-b866184.html

government, most notably Matt Hancock. He was Secretary of State for Health and Social Care when he was caught in intimate acts with his own secretary which his own directives barred the British people from engaging in with people outside their 'household' or 'bubble.'

His family promptly blew up and he has most recently begged to return to politics for the sake of his own financial solubility having run off with his mistress. He is still an MP, though I hope not for long.

You'd think it would stop here, that people in positions of power so vaunted as the British Parliament would show some respect for their constituents, even if out of purely Machiavellian desire to advance their station by appearing squeaky clean, never mind basic decency.

You'd be wrong.

Professor Neil Ferguson, key government advisor, met a lover at his house on the 5th of May 2020 and resigned after subsequent exposure.

The PM's own father was insulated against rule-breaking by a mere apology, whilst others were prosecuted in court and sometimes handed out bank-breaking fines. Nepotism at its finest; that phrase would also be another contender for how to describe Johnson's career in one sentence. A lower Secretary, Mr Robert Jenrick, also broke rules making a 150 mile journey to Hertfordshire, to no consequence.[124]

---

[124] *From Corbyn to Cummings, the public figures who have broken Covid rules.* (2020, October 2). The Independent. https://www.independent.co.uk/news/uk/home-news/coronavirus-lockdown-rules-dominic-cummings-robert-jenrick-stephen-kinnock-stanley-johnson-b745344.html

How Lockdown Itself violates any Model of Consistent Law

Consider what would happen if everybody obeyed lockdowns.

If this were the case, if everyone ceased all movement and interaction with others, not only would the economy completely collapse, but for the purposes of our model, COVID transmissions would drop to zero or near enough.

So we would, for the period of the lockdown, be trapped in a state of limbo with zero transmission and economic mayday. One will see the problem with how carrying this policy out to its logical apex defeats its own object; to reduce transmission to a manageable rate.

Assuming the virus remains viably transmissible after our theoretical perfect lockdown, once it was lifted, we would see a repeat of the autumnal spikes in infection and reproduction rates, only far, far worse as, assuming that this perfect lockdown kicked in early and no vaccine would be developed in time, as was the case for the first lockdown and the tiered one too, near none of the population would be immune.

Now, contrast the actual lockdown policy to this ideal. Sold around slogans of 'three weeks to flatten the curve',[125] one is left with two ways of working the lockdown if it is not to simply delay infection across time without actually protecting the population against the virus as a force.

These are either, to assume that a certain amount of people will defy the rules, changing across time, and this will modulate

---

[125] *The Longest Three Weeks in History—From "Flattening the Curve" to a Permanent "New Abnormal."* (2021, February 16). Astute News. https://astutenews.com/2021/02/the-longest-three-weeks-in-history-from-flattening-the-curve-to-a-permanent-new-abnormal/?cn-reloaded=1

infection rates as well as providing some start to immunity, or, expose people by certain demographics at a time. The UK took a hybrid approach between these two models.

The first assumption, that some people will violate a given law, is a valid one. Such is the premise on which criminal law, at least its punitive element, is largely based.

However, it is one thing for a law to account for people breaking it in its own design.

It's another for the law itself to depend on its own being broken in order to function.

Fines are perhaps one example of a law which functions by that self-defeating model; it's often made more of an issue in the U.S. where funding for police is handled differently and there is a profit incentive behind prosecution.

Lockdown policies take this to another level.

If one assumes that they were to work based on people breaking them, one has, as before, defined a law which must be broken to achieve its own intended objective.

This seems anathema to any model of consistent law. After all, the remainder of the corpus of law, at least as far as I understand it, is designed and agreed upon precisely because it is agreed, at least by some figure of those with the relevant power in the polity, that the law in question should not be broken.

This lockdown model therefore, stands as an aberration to the model of the law as something to be respected and obeyed.

I speak of the law generally and conceptually—certainly there are unjust laws in specific cases and one may also argue that the framing of the law within a monopolist on organised violence is unjust by nature.

However, we must remember context.

These laws were brought in by a Conservative government. A government which supposedly champions 'law and order'. For a law to be ordered, it presumably must be obeyed or regarded at least that it should be obeyed in most circumstances.

Theorists of jurisprudence have based entire fields of study on this presupposition, from Hart to Dworkin to Simmonds.

Yet, under this model, in order for lockdowns to have the effect of spreading the burden of the COVID pandemic across time, they have to be disobeyed by their subjects to some degree, or they would simply delay the inevitable.

Hence, lockdowns as legally modelled do grave damage to any concept of sanctity of the law. This is supposedly a concept which a Conservative government would treasure.

Except, of course, when it gets in the way of political convenience...

Lockdowns as Unjust Discrimination

There is an alternative model however, which the UK also attempted to use. It can be divided into two further categories.

This model, as a whole, would run to categorise lockdowns by their exposure of certain sections or demographics within the population to the virus, a given number at a time, so as to place the strain in predictable areas ahead of time.

The first way this manifested, and the first of the two categories into which this model can be divided, is the idea of a 'key worker.' For those outside the UK, these were teachers, emergency workers and some other professions who were either permitted or obliged, depending on their economic situation, to keep working through the lockdown.

This might, initially, seem a sensible proposition; it's hardly worth spending extortionate amounts of the public purse on show hospitals if there's nobody around to work in them.

However, there is a far more insidious element to this framing.

We must ask ourselves the question asked by every sceptic

across history—who gets to define the subject and will any bias or perverse incentive affect either that definition or actions taken further ahead in time after it?

In short, who gets to define 'key worker'?

In this instance, it was the First Johnson Ministry.

Now, putting aside other objections, the first thing which becomes immediately obvious is that this arrangement only works so far as the Johnson Ministry and its definition of what is key and what is not to the nation on a macrological level.

For a people so often cynical about their overlords, we Brits put a lot of implicit faith in them to determine who was key and who was not just by tolerating this definition. This is one aspect which I fail to commune with my countrymen on; they will happily complain about their parasitic overlords for hours on end, whilst doing nothing about it. I will never understand this.

The contrast hints at the second objection; by their complacency, the British populace have now allowed their government to say whose labour is more important than whose, subject to no balance or criterion than their own revelation, regret and reticence.

The dangers of this should be immediately obvious; statistical aggregates and broad-stroke categorisations cannot possibly hope to encompass the nuance of the situation of every family and worker in the UK. It is not for the government to know what work is key to which person per Hayek's Local Knowledge Problem,[126] nor for them to say, per freedom of association.

Some may reply: 'well, only in a crisis!'

I will bet any sum of money these people like, that this

---

[126] Hayek, F. (1945). *The Use of Knowledge in Society*, The American Economic Review, *35*(4), 519–530.
https://german.yale.edu/sites/default/files/hayek_-_the_use_of_knowledge_in_society.pdf

precedent will be expanded beyond this instance, no matter how tacitly. Where people tell a government: 'We concede that you can use power x, but only in a time of crisis', history and a basic understanding of human nature both show that there is a painfully obvious incentive for a government to then either manufacture a crisis to gain access to those powers or use an already occurring crisis to invoke those powers, even where the two may not be related. These range in scale and severity, the USS Maine, Reichstag Fire and 9/11 all come to mind alongside this pandemic as examples of where this incentive has applied.

History will be replete with many more to even the most cursory examination if that number is insufficient. What the idea of a government determined key worker has created, is a precedent where that government can institutionalise discrimination, real discrimination, between labourers on account of nothing more than its own thoughts on them, not their needs, abilities, or with any other check or balance on that government's ability to do so beyond the overrated and inequitable power of the vote.

This line of thinking, should it be abused, has the potential to be devastating to its victims, as the events of the 80's clearly showed—and that wasn't the government actively deciding that miners no longer mattered so much as passively taking the industry off of unaffordable life support.

Imagine how much worse a modern version of those events would be where the government actively decided that a certain sector was undesirable, and used this new precedent to take action, with so many more lives, both present and future, dependent on industries now more than ever woven together by financial vehicles.

George Beglan

Lockdowns as a Danger to the Principles behind *Habeus Corpus* and wider Legal Protections

Some definitions will suit our purposes at the outset.

Habeus corpus is, most fundamentally, both a prerogative writ and a recourse at law. The first term means that it is an order from one organ of government directing another. The second means that it is a solution for a problem a party, person or corporation, is experiencing at law.

Its effect is to order a detainer to produce someone in their (the ordered body's) detention before a court at a given time and place. Normally, this is to review if the detention in question is lawful. One sees the first limitation of it in this case immediately— in and of itself it's nothing more than an organ of the law. It is a writ of right, not course, so it is only a procedural remedy.

This is to say that, though it may protect people against whatever detention is unlawful, if the law permits all detention, the writ has no effect. It only has effect as far as permitted within its own legal framework.

As such, it will not do to argue that *habeus corpus* in and of itself, as writ or doctrine, constitutes a protection against lockdowns or is violated at law by them.

Indeed, if one was to confine this discussion to the law itself, there would be little to discuss. Procedure of the law is subject to the law itself and as such, the Coronavirus Act 2020 would eliminate any *habeus corpus* concerns on its own procedure, as would every other law.

This immediately shows the next objection; if discussion of *habeus corpus* in and of the law is limited to the present constitution of the law, one must look to the principles behind its inception and their application to the present facts. The only other alternative is logical circularity and insisting that the law as presently constituted is the sum of the material to be discussed, which would be absurd.

So, what were the guiding principles behind writ and doctrine? Most commonly, it is traced to the Assize of Clarendon during the reign of Henry II during the 12th century with the following words:

> *No Freeman shall be taken or imprisoned, or be disseized of his Freehold, or Liberties, or free Customs, or be outlawed, or exiled, or any other wise destroyed; nor will We not pass upon him, nor condemn him, but by lawful judgment of his Peers, or by the Law of the land.*

This started a legal revolution later reaffirmed in the Magna Carta, which is often incorrectly cited as the incepting document of the doctrine. The law has evolved to its current situation of circularity and this itself may seem to be reaffirmed by the words of the Assize, especially the final two clauses.

On the other hand, it is also clear that the moral aims informing this law are the preservation of liberty and freedom.

Moreover, the Assize was based upon contemporaneous evidential practice which was far more binary—one did not conceptualise of 'potential murderers' or 'potential thieves' in 12th century law, there was no doctrine of inchoate crimes and nothing of the surveillance apparatus around today.

Yet the Coronavirus Act 2020 speaks openly and gladly of 'potentially infectious individuals', without retaining any requirement that the individuals in question be proved as infectious.

It would be disingenuous to speak of the doctrine as

unassailable. It has been suspended multiple times throughout British history.

However, the danger of allowing the passage of bills such as the Coronavirus Act may be far more insidiously dangerous than a simple suspension; the presumption is that, once the circumstances causing the suspension have abated, the doctrine in question will be restored without backdoor edition whilst it was disapplied. This is the presumption, irrespective of how true it may end up being.

However, allowing the treatment of all 'potentially infectious' persons as those potentially and validly targetable by the state's monopoly on violence damages a corollary of *habeus corpus* in a far more stealthy manner.

It, in practice, reverses the burden of proof, which formerly lay on the state. That is to say, the detaining organ of the state, in the event that *habeus corpus* was to be invoked, had to show that its detention complied with both writ and doctrine.

At law, this situation may remain unchanged.

However, let us examine the statutory wording under Schedule 1 of the Coronavirus Act:

Potentially infectious persons

1. For the purposes of this Schedule, a person is "potentially infectious" at any time if—

   the person is, or may be, infected or contaminated with coronavirus, and there is a risk that the person might infect or contaminate others with coronavirus, or

   the person has been in an infected area within the 14 days preceding that time.

2. For the purposes of this paragraph, "infected area"

means any country, territory or other area outside the United Kingdom which the Secretary of State has declared as a country, territory or area—

where there is known or thought to be sustained human-to-human transmission of coronavirus, or

from which there is a high risk that coronavirus will be transmitted to the United Kingdom.

The Schedule later goes on to elaborate about the new powers to detain individuals who fall into the above definition, such as to move people to 'places suitable for [COVID] testing', powers suitable to be exercised at these places, and most disturbingly, according to Paragraph 14(2):

3. *A public health officer may at any time during the transmission control period impose such requirements and restrictions on the person as the officer considers necessary and proportionate—*

in the interests of the person,

for the protection of other people, or

(c) for the maintenance of public health.

This measure is not let to bring totality against the undesirable infected alone—the next Paragraph outlines sunset protocols, that the impositions not exceed 14 days, that a public health officer review the decision within 48 hours of an appointment, so on.

However, the act also makes clear that it's not just infected people subject to this, but also any people whose status is 'inconclusive.'

This inconclusiveness is again, predictably, seconded to a 'public health officer', who must decide the matter concerning a novel virus which they lack total comprehension of by their own admission. This is especially relevant by virtue of the contest and debate over exactly how COVID-19's infectivity varies with circumstances such as masking, vaccination and so on, which, to the distant observer and, crucially, lawyers, actuaries and police officers who lack medical education, might seem far from settled.

In some way it might be said, and many lockdown worshippers have presupposed their argument upon, it being unknown if the entire population was potentially infectious, or if every single person in it constituted a potential vector for infection.

Take this argument and apply it to the above statute.

The resulting implication is that, should the lockdown worshippers have their way, to be counted as a free citizen exempt from the summary removal of your liberties, one would have to prove a lack of infectivity, in the face of imperfectly accurate tests, and especially marked macrological issues in the UK with testing procedure.

The principles which informed habeas corpus are forgotten, trampled under the demand for public purity from a virus which no reasonable person would consistently say is sufficiently poor conduct to constitute criminality, at least under any conventionally understood criminal burden of proof.

Moreover, the doctrine itself becomes toothless at law, present *de jure* but defanged *de facto* by the demand that you prove your purity to the Leviathan before it dignify you with your supposed rights.

Does your fellow citizen engage in harming you by negligence by daring to go outside when they have a common flu or cold? Multiple authorities the worshippers themselves point to have made clear that we will eventually have to treat COVID like those very same seasonal infections.

If your answer was no, I challenge you to find an intellectually consistent way to justify the response to COVID, i.e., one which doesn't boil down to: 'But it's an emergency, you callous freedom lover!'

Will Her Majesty's Opposition Please Stand Up?

Parliamentary opposition to lockdowns since the exit of Jeremy Corbyn from the Labour Party has been, for all intents and purposes, non-existent at worst and ineffectual at best.

One might think that the clue is in the name, especially for those outside the UK.

You might presume that Her Majesty's Honourable Opposition would do just that, oppose government policy.

Wishful thinking.

This book will not seek to defend Corbyn, or comment on him outside its scope, but from his statements on the matter it does seem that he would have been a stronger opponent of these policies than current leader Sir Keir Starmer, if for very different reasons than the author might like. This least of all from his speech at the 'Kill the Bill' protests against the priorly discussed Police and Crime Bill—the first time in living memory the author found himself agreeing with something Corbyn had to say.

Criticism of Sir Keir might not earn many favours at this stage; many will doubtless argue that the COVID pandemic has overshadowed any unique flavour he might have brought to the opposition and forced him to take up a certain position in response to it. They would then argue, at best guess, that it would be best to allow some return to normality before passing judgment.

It is my submission however, that the exact opposite is true.

Times of crisis should be, if anything, the moment where the opposition must stand most resolute of all, precisely to prevent, or at the very least impose a price upon, the very expansion of government power and hypocrisy in exercising it discussed throughout this chapter.

Governments of national unity and collaborative oppositions might be pleasing to one's aesthetic taste or to some ideal of unity but are a recipe for disaster if one desires to keep the state in check.

This disaster, has been exactly what is observed throughout the COVID-19 pandemic in the UK through the policy of the Starmer Opposition.

Starmer notably came into the role of Leader of the Opposition on the claim that he 'would not politicise the pandemic'.[127] This statement, regrettably, remained true for all of two weeks. It wasn't long before the succour of Prime Minister's Questions (PMQ's), a television broadcast debate every week where the Prime Minister or some emissary for them is held to account in front of Parliament, made Starmer into another political hack selecting points which happened to drive home party agenda on the tv screen. Whilst this was happening, Labour MP's wrote large voted with the government to extend the tyrannical powers of the Coronavirus Act every time. It was only Conservative rebels who, in large part, constituted any Parliamentary opposition. Sometimes the hypocrisy of these actions was so painfully self-evident that only a thoroughbred Parliamentarian could possibly perform the mental gymnastics necessary to justify them.

---

[127] Wax, E. (2020, April 5). *Keir Starmer vows to work "constructively" with UK government on coronavirus.* POLITICO. https://www.politico.eu/article/keir-starmer-vows-to-work-constructively-with-uk-government-on-coronavirus/

The Right to Protest, gone extinct?

The spring of 2021 in the UK, just as lockdown policies were beginning to be repealed, came not with a whisper, but a scream. The tragic rape and murder of a young woman, Sarah Everard, by a former Metropolitan Police Officer, swiftly grabbed national headlines and seized hold of the public *zeitgeist*. Labour and left-wing parties across the UK were very quick to appeal to their feminist elements on the back of these events in lieu of justice in courts of law, with some going so far as to echo support for a motion in the U.S. to bring in a curfew only applying to men.

Equal protection before the law was out, the sisterhood *uber allus* was in.

Laws were also going before Parliament at the same time regulating the right to protest. These laws, at least as presently constituted, are dangerously vague, allowing the censure of any protest which poses a 'significant disturbance or annoyance.'

Disregarding that this is the entire point of a civil protest, there came, for a period of about a week before the Second Reading of the bill in Parliament (the reading where most serious debate of the bill happens) an increased spike in activism to preserve the right to protest in the face of this bill.

Miraculously it seemed, left-wing activists suddenly cared about liberty and regrew a moral compass, despite being the very same people to scream at those defying lockdowns as selfish murderers when doing so wouldn't involve angering their feminist overlords. The fact that this happened just when it was fashionable to virtue signal about this cause, is and was of course, nothing more than happy coincidence...

Whatever the drive for involvement, the day before the reading of the bill, protests across the UK became violent—some in London but far more noticeably (at least on account of the mainstream media covering only this instance) in Bristol.

Bristol is a city with a strong left-wing tradition and, fittingly, one which entered international headlines during the worldwide BLM protests.

It did so because, for those of you living under a rock, local residents toppled a statute of colonial slave trader and benefactor Edward Coulston, before throwing it into the local harbour.

A spring of copycat petitions and movements across the UK enjoyed brief surges in popularity, most notably Rhodes Must Fall in Oxford, which insists that a man of similar stature and statue, Cecil Rhodes, must be removed from the face of Oriel College, and presumably the renaming of his scholarship which helps bring disadvantaged students to the university.

They were, last I checked, defeated by of all things, red tape planning regulation concerning the modification of listed buildings, but we shall see how events continue to unfold.

If one wanted to allow radical activists from any political element temporary control of a given city in order to show to the world the folly of their ideas, one might say that Bristol is the UK's Seattle and CHAZ—a second order city not sufficiently close to the heartland that protest would demand immediate reaction from central government, but sufficiently well known that violence within its bounds could be used to make a point.

Combine with the priorly discussed political history, and you have something of a prime target for a scapegoat. I'm not arguing that there was necessarily any government involvement in either inciting or planning the events prior to the passage of the bill, I lack the evidence to make that argument and am not a conspiracy theorist.

One would be remiss to mention that such intervention, however Machiavellian, is not unheard of (though again, much more a problem in the U.S. than the UK) and given the recent history along with the politically relevant position of Bristol, one could not think of a better place to make an example of: 'if you don't pass our bill, this could happen in your constituency'…

For whatever its worth to you dear reader, my instinct says that it's all a little too well-timed to be just a coincidence, especially with the Bristol mayor stating that the rioters within the city on that night were probably not residents.

Either that or, I have truly underestimated the rioters' stupidity and deafness to tragic irony; it would have been obvious that their actions would immediately be used to demonstrate the necessity of the very bill they were protesting.

It seems likely as of the time of writing that this bill will pass and the right to protest in the UK significantly damaged as a result. The Labour Party voted almost unilaterally against, to their credit.

Vaccine Authoritarianism in the UK—Diseases and Authoritarianism; is COVID just a Cultural Microcosm?

Some readers will no doubt be aware of Professor Jordan B Peterson.

To some a figure of controversy, to others, a father they never had and to most, perhaps, somewhere in between. This book will not discuss his character or other elements, but rather one the more minor recurring themes within his lecture series which may otherwise go unnoticed and is particularly relevant to the topic of this book.

Peterson divides the question of how to graph political alignment into a question of borders: 'Should there be borders and if so, how strict should they be?'—one's answer to this master key question would, in his model, indicate one's political alignment with a high degree of accuracy.

Frequent watchers of his may have osmosed the knowledge that there is a strong correlation between the prevalence of parasites in a community and that community's acceptance of authoritarian politics and social management.[128]

This is not an exact match for viral transmission of disease but the theme and question remains—what exactly is the relationship between people's acceptance of authoritarian politics and their own public health? Furthermore, if it could be proven, as Dr Peterson suggested in a blog post,[129] that one method of eradicating authoritarianism would be the improvement of public health, that the inverse could also be true? Could it be true that, if infectious diseases were to re-emerge, perhaps through any medium rather than just parasites, one would observe a similar surge in authoritarianism?

The question definitely seems worth asking in the UK.

The Johnson Ministry has not just lied to the British people, but has presided over the greatest slide towards authoritarianism in liberty's former home for generations. This is shown most clearly in the Coronavirus Act 2020 and the new Policing Bill. I would argue, though this has been met with great trepidation at my own law faculty, that specifically Section 51[130] of that Coronavirus Act and the corresponding Schedule 21,[131] which concerns: 'Powers relating to potentially infectious persons' goes so far as to contradict if not outright endanger the doctrine of *habeus corpus*.

But yet, bills like the Investigatory Powers Act 2016, which

---

[128] Murray, D. R., Schaller, M., & Suedfeld, P. (2013). *Pathogens and Politics: Further Evidence That Parasite Prevalence Predicts Authoritarianism.* PLoS ONE, *8*(5), e62275.
https://doi.org/10.1371/journal.pone.0062275
[129] Peterson, J. (2020, May 25). *Infectious Disease and Authoritarianism.* Www.thinkspot.com.
https://www.thinkspot.com/discourse/RkuyRn/post/jordan-peterson/infectious-disease-and-authoritarianism/b6mtwx#
[130] Coronavirus Act 2020, 51. Retrieved April 3, 2021 from:
https://www.legislation.gov.uk/ukpga/2020/7/section/51/enacted
[131] Ibid. p 21.

set the tone for this legislation, were not made in the backdrop of a pandemic. There seems then, something more to it, as one would always expect in sociology.

Most disturbingly of all, these calls seem to be persisting beyond the supposed vaccine-cure for COVID-19. The Netherlands has, of the time of writing, suspended deployment of the Oxford AstraZeneca vaccine for under-60's over fears of its inducing of blood clots.[132] This fear seems largely overblown,[133] so we should not dismiss vaccines as a cure on the current evidence.

Why then, does fear persist?

It seems to not be enough to Johnson that the UK have some of the most effective vaccination programs in Europe, to the point where the EU threatened to block exports vital to its continuing, seemingly out of nought but jealousy, spite and bitterness on the part of one Ursula von de Leyen.[134]

No, one must prove vaccination, or some other method of immunity or non-risk, to be a Briton beyond mere name. The supposed goal of turning the British people into livestock to be tagged is to 'provide businesses certainty.[135]

---

[132] Crisp, J. (2021, April 2). *Netherlands suspends AstraZeneca Covid vaccine for under-60s*. The Telegraph. https://www.telegraph.co.uk/news/2021/04/02/netherlands-suspends-astrazeneca-covid-vaccine-under-60s/

[133] Gallagher, J. (2021, April 2). *AstraZeneca: Is there a blood clot risk?* BBC News. https://www.bbc.co.uk/news/health-56594189

[134] Blewett, S. (2021, March 17). *EU threatens to halt coronavirus vaccine exports to UK*. Www.standard.co.uk. https://www.standard.co.uk/news/uk/ursula-von-der-leyen-astrazeneca-european-commission-boris-johnson-pfizer-b924686.html

[135] Live, T. (2021, March 25). *PM Boris Johnson explains how Covid passports could work*. TeessideLive. https://www.gazettelive.co.uk/news/teesside-news/boris-johnson-explains-how-covid-20252956

We mustn't kid ourselves, this is nothing new; the explicit idea of citizens being mere cattle of the Leviathan before all else dates back to Westphalia at the latest and the broader theme permeates human history near totally.

Surely though, if the pandemic has proven anything, it is that the grim reaping Johnson Ministry should only provide businesses certainty in one way.

That is by getting its perfumed nose out of the books of those who remain following the Great Lockdown Purge and never coming back. Businesses' own competitors, who may accept custom with or without vaccine unless proscribed at law, provides certainty by discipline of constant dealings. Either cast your sales net as wide as possible, or be out-competed.

The previously noted article outlines the reticence of business owners in the very field the 'vaccine passport' is supposed to protect on the policy. This at least, is what would happen in standard economic theory.

Aside from this, one questions exactly why it is that the Johnson Ministry keeps revising lockdown policies and seemingly desires to keep them in effect for far longer than those elsewhere.

Perhaps it feels that the promise during the third lockdown that once removed, lockdowns would not be returning, was premature on the facts and politically far too costly to reside on. If one was to follow the U.S. as a model, one might move back to some kind of tier system or resign the idea to lower boards of governance. This idea was however, struck off.[136].

Yet despite the success of vaccines throughout the first third of 2021, and the variance of the prevalence of COVID, and those

---

[136] Toufexi, I. (2021, February 22). *"England won't return to tiers after lockdown"* *says* *vaccines* *minister.* CambridgeshireLive. https://www.cambridge-news.co.uk/news/uk-world-news/boris-johnson-roadmap-plan-england-19886125

vaccines across the country, there is a continued insistence from the One-Nationists that the issue be treated unilaterally.

The internal tension of this decision with the prior use of a system of tiers which discriminated by the prevalence of the virus in localities is obvious—are we treating the virus with acknowledgment of local differences, or not?

One fears the political incentive to not do so—with by-elections still ongoing and specific targeting of seats highly likely to be an opposition strategy, inspiring envy in those still under lockdown by removing restrictions early for parts of the nation still doing well would be a dangerous political strategy, if also being the honest thing to do.

Tier systems were also, by public sentiment, largely unpopular. That last part may also be the most dangerous part of the increased vaccine authoritarianism—that public sentiment will affirm it come the next election.

Inroads into liberty are seldom made with dramatic flair and immediately huge damage.

Those who have attempted such things have often found themselves signalling far too much aggression to those under their thumb and have been made to pay for it.

Each Caesar should beware his Ides of March.

Peoples do however surrender their rights slowly, to arguments which are labelled as 'common sense' or 'empathic' when they are often anything but. Such has been the argument for many advocating for lockdowns.

That it is about saving lives, despite the overwhelming counter-point that is Sweden and that as such to even dare challenge the motion is to be callous. In the alternative, that this scenario is a crisis and as such exceptional infringements on rights are granted. Not only does this obviously violate any consistent model of rights as already discussed, but it also creates the incentive already discussed for governments to manufacture such crises.

Further, diseases with a far higher mortality rate than COVID-19 have not been met with such a brutish response. SARS, itself caused by a different kind of Coronavirus, has a fatality rate of three, going on four times that of COVID-19, comparing the most recent figures, yet it wasn't treated with such broad strokes.[137]

Only Mexico comes close in terms of a comparable death rate, according to Johns Hopkins[138]. Perhaps the initial nebulosity of COVID-19 as it spread out of China was what scared governments into initial lockdowns, and they then felt compelled to defend this faulty policy by non-virtue of costs already sunk into it.

A further microcosm of COVID-19 authoritarianism emerged recently.

YouTube recently removed all advertising revenue from the channel of conservative commentator Steven Crowder for daring to so much as present proof from the WHO's own statistics which might challenge the idea of lockdown being a good policy.[139] The same WHO that, despite their own internally inconsistent advice and statements, are apparently the foremost authority on the

---

[137] Chan-Yeung, M., & Xu, R.-H. (2003). SARS: epidemiology. *Respirology (Carlton, Vic.), 8 Suppl,* S9-14.
https://doi.org/10.1046/j.1440-1843.2003.00518.x
[138] Hopkins, J. (2021). MORTALITY ANALYSES. In *Johns Hopkins University & Medicine.*
https://coronavirus.jhu.edu/data/mortality
[139] Hollister, S. (2021, March 30). *YouTube has removed Steven Crowder from its Partner Program indefinitely.* The Verge. https://www.theverge.com/2021/3/30/22359191/steven-crowder-youtube-partner-program-suspension-demonetize-ads-strike-ban-misinformation

matter.[140]

Psalm 115:3 comes to mind, with some of my own modification:

> But our God is in the Heavens, _he does whatever_
> _he pleases_ [and should you even dare attempt to
> discuss him in a way we, clear monopolists of moral
> authority and society find displeasing, all woe
> betide you.]

This is where we observe the most dangerous phenomenon which seems to be creeping into Western discourse.

It is not simply 'cancel culture', now far too overreaching a term, applicable across far too many instances, to point to this phenomenon specifically. After all, one can be cancelled for many things, the mob is capricious and cares little for self-moderation, as has been tragically revealed in many cases.

More specifically and terrifyingly, there now seems to be some critical mass behind the idea that we bar evidence supporting any view we do not like entirely from discussion.

That we selectively ignore fact where we dislike it in preference of such things as feelings or even a predominant social narrative.

People bias towards this kind of behaviour and pattern of thought naturally—we are not perfectly rational Bayesian belief-updating machines.

However, the solipsistic stance of elevating this phenomenon from a bias to be eradicated into an epistemic policy used to

---

[140] Kuo, L. (2020, June 2). _China withheld data on coronavirus from WHO, recordings reveal._ The Guardian. https://www.theguardian.com/world/2020/jun/02/china-withheld-data-coronavirus-world-health-organization-recordings-reveal

maintain delusion seems to be a good indicator of the state of political discourse more generally.

Think of anytime you hear the revolting phrase 'my truth' as an immediately accessible example. This seems to be the way YouTube behaved toward Crowder. This is the way the majority of people my own age seem to think about Sweden's handling of COVID-19—they find some way to except it from their models, and then don't think any further.

My generation and their immediate predecessors have rendered culture at large such that God is no longer love, love (or whatever the loudest plurality says is love, irrespective of the facts) is god, and any dissent or scepticism of a policy or body identified with that goal becomes, by that faux, engineered definition, hatred.

This discussion may wander dangerously close to some mix of epistemology and polemics, and the author's views on objective philosophy over subjective would be largely outside the purview of this book; so allow me to summate the necessary parts and argue that I form an extremely tentative view, mindful of my own limitations and ignorance, on the basis of applying Occam's Razor to the scenario.

If I have understood the rationalists, logic or philosophy wrote whole correctly, subjectivism must imply the need for a thing to be experienced by its lens to some degree in order to function.

Even if one takes this to its logical extreme of solipsism and asserts the self as the only thing, there must be some *grundnorm* by which the self can be compared to the other not—things for that assertion to have any meaning.

The inverse is not necessarily true, if one assumes that mathematics, or perhaps more accurately, the things which mathematics describe, remain a fundamental law and aspect of the universe irrespective of the human experience.

Subjective experience therefore depends on something

relatively objective (the thing in question) to experience or compare against, an objective description of that thing does not. Hence, objective philosophies explain the same phenomenon by reference to fewer variables and should be preferred, *ceteris paribus*.

I mention this to point to the cultural contrast.

This apparently, is not how we are supposed to think today. Increasingly, from both sides of the traditional statist political spectrum, the promotion of ignorance seems to be on the rise—lunacies such as 'alternative facts,'[141] on one side, 'my truth and my reality' on the other.

There remains some hope.

It is possible, looking at the spreadsheets, that we are seeing the decline of a centralised mainstream media, and the furore which seems to have manifested since 2016, is a twin product of its failing to acquire the best talent and a lack of any dependence on direct viewership.

Where the media are state-sponsored, such as in the case of the BBC, they can depend on an emotional public more than willing to act as host to its utterly non-viable and therefore parasitic system in a market economy.

In the case of corporatists, many lobbyists for networks like CNN and FOX, are now so well married into advertising and politics that the money may well continue to flow regardless of how viewership behaves, within certain parameters.

If the decentralised internet was to challenge this model of

---

[141] Blake, A. (2017, January 22). *Kellyanne Conway says Donald Trump's team has 'alternative facts.' Which pretty much says it all.* The Washington Post.
https://www.washingtonpost.com/news/the-fix/wp/2017/01/22/kellyanne-conway-says-donald-trumps-team-has-alternate-facts-which-pretty-much-says-it-all/

operation, why do its executives behave so similarly? Twitter is by far the worst offender (I do not have an account with them, nor do I suspect I ever will), violating its own policies on clarity and content moderation.[142]

This remains true even after its executives were summoned before Congress (though the hearing in question was painfully obvious point scoring.)

Others do too however, Amazon arguably acted in an anti-trusting or anti-competitive manner by deplatforming Parler[143] and Facebook has come under fire too.[144]

Perhaps then, all we are seeing is no more than technological innovation combined with fundamental laws of market structure—people are drawn to these platforms because of the lower cost and greater possibilities associated with them—all you need is an internet connection to forge your own narrative, rather than needing a TV to at best reinterpret one given to you. Oligopolists within the market then promote their own views because they have the market share required to do so.

There is debate over just how deliberate this is, whether its explicitly given from high office, as seems to be the case with

---

[142] Kirchoff, C. (2021, March 26). *Twitter Suspends Steven Crowder's Account AGAIN. Still No Reason Given!* Louder with Crowder. https://www.louderwithcrowder.com/twitter-suspends-steven-crowders-account-again-still-no-reason-given

[143] Williams, J. (2021, January 11). *Parler Files Antitrust Suit Against Amazon After Server Suspension.* Courthouse News Service. https://www.courthousenews.com/parler-files-antitrust-suit-against-amazon-after-server-suspension/

[144] International, T. K. S. (2016, June 17). *Age of Deplatforming: Short List of Conservative Voices Muted by Internet Giants.* Sputniknews.com. https://sputniknews.com/society/202006171079643572-age-of-deplatforming-short-list-of-conservative-voices-muted-by-internet-giants/

Disney, or whether these firms are composed almost exclusively of fresh-eyed collectivists just out of drawing strings and so a labour sampling bias manifests in their output I find it so impossible to relate to.

Whatever the case, we: you and I dear reader, must fight this cultural descent into authoritarianism and gangster politics.

We seem outgunned, if not also outnumbered, at least for now.

So I charge you, if resisting this growing cancer in our culture appeals to you, you must become an army in your own right. As before, we can defeat the authoritarians on the facts, we can defeat them by reference to history, we can defeat them by their own logically illiterate standards.

All that must be deciphered is how to sell our positions to a people less happy than ever, and to, as before, not take one step back.

The Fashionable Bigotry of the 'Woke' and its link to Vaccine Authoritarianism

In practice, we may see the unvaccinated being turned into this generation's fashionable *Untermensch*, despite how many of my generation would furiously deny any discriminatory tendencies on their own part.

This is especially true given that, on so called 'freedom day' of July 19th, the government stated its further expectation that explicit proof of a vaccine against COVID, not just a negative test would be a necessary precondition to entry to areas where 'large crowds gather', such as nightclubs.[145]

---

[145] Wheeler, R. (2021, July 19). *Proof of vaccination to be required for entry to nightclubs from autumn.* Www.msn.com. https://www.msn.com/en-us/news/world/proof-of-vaccination-to-be-required-for-entry-to-nightclubs-from-autumn/ar-AAMkaac

At the time of writing, some 35% of 18-30-year-olds were unvaccinated—some 3 million people. It seems then, that on the Johnson government's view, it is an acceptable preservation of liberty and principle to simply treat those who disagree with your utility analysis as regards vaccination as undesirables to be shunned, or coerce their consent to the vaccine, right to bodily autonomy be damned.

Further, it is actively desirable policy to mobilise your monopoly on organised violence to compel defenceless third party private enterprises, businesses into enforcing that shunning.

All the better to make it seem a societal norm.

Charming behaviour from a man who wanted to avoid his own laws when they applied to him and the last few remaining sycophants, only backing down when that avoidance seemed to dent his popularity.[146]

I warn you now, dear reader, it is policies like this, designed to disallow debate and turn decisions fundamental to your humanity into a technocratic exercise which will open the door to a more subtle and far more dangerous kind of tyranny.

Perhaps not the kind where oppression is openly recognisable, though that is a ready possibility. At least that brand can be openly decried and fought.

This kind of resilement of decision by government, its mobilising to mob you of your agency, opens the door to a far more fundamental tyranny where one does not recognise, or sympathises with, one's own oppression. See the gradual

---

[146] Quinn, B., Syal, R., & Topham, G. (2021, July 18). *Questions grow over pilot scheme after Johnson and Sunak isolation U-turn.* The Guardian.
https://www.theguardian.com/politics/2021/jul/18/questions-grow-pilot-scheme-boris-johnson-rishi-sunak-covid-self-isolation-u-turn

infringement on financial liberty in the United States over the course of its history, culminating in the Sixteenth Amendment and the entrenchment of the Federal Reserve into the framework of the nation.

Yeonmi Park, North Korean defector, and a woman who should be treated as a Delphian Oracle rather than the Oresteian Cassandra she seems to be treated as by the modern left, puts the point beautifully,[147] that the truest oppression is that which cannot be seen because it is not recognised as such; it becomes that which is chosen or defaulted to because the defenseless are raised to believe that it is the only option.

I do not deny the effectiveness of the vaccines.

Individual benefits of receiving a vaccine do not mismatch the benefits other people derive from you taking a vaccine, especially if they are linked to deaths. Those deaths are immensely rare, almost statistically irrelevant.

However, if one assumes that one's own death is an infinitely negative utility loss from one's own point of view, which seems a safe assumption to me, Pascal's Wager is then engaged, and at that stage the technocrats receive the burden of either escaping or defeating the Wager.

For the uninitiated, the Wager is a philosophical argument originally used to argue that even if there one thinks it most likely that there isn't a God, one should still behave as if there is, but its core logic can be expanded to any situation where non-zero probabilities of both finite and infinite utility gain or loss (finite gain in the case of a successful vaccine, infinite loss in the case of a

---

[147] Campbell, N. (2021, June 21). *"People Choose To Be Brainwashed" Says North Korean Defector on Her Experience at US Ivy League School,* Vision Times. Www.visiontimes.com. https://www.visiontimes.com/2021/06/21/north-korean-yeonmi-park-columbia.html

vaccine which kills you) have to be compared.

If I dare wager my own argument, the technocrats awareness of difficulties like this is why they are so keen to use social engineering to 'nudge' you towards vaccination and, of course, in a complete coincidence not at all engineered, the resiling of your own research and critical thought on your own decisions towards them, increasing their power.

It is also why they absolutely refuse to even engage in debate, defaulting to nonarguments about their own self-appointed status as expert—the bizarre lie that the correct series of letters after your name makes what you say right, rather than its truth and, failing that 'common sense', the byword of all those who cannot express their arguments with sufficient clarity to be overwhelm opposition and so appeal to base instinct.

The last thing an expert should do, surely?

Further discussion of vaccines is not my purview and from my limited knowledge, they seem phenomenally effective for how rapidly they were produced. However, my generation, and to a large extent the one before us, has always looked down on those who refused to vaccinate either themselves or their children since Andrew Wakefield disgraced himself over the MMR vaccine.[148]

Labelling those who refuse vaccines as uneducated or irresponsible is often the kindest thing said of them. Many are conspiracy theorists with no credibility, true enough. But one worries about the risk of over-correction.

Think I'm overreacting?

Ask yourself, dear reader, when was the last time you bothered to entertain any kind, or an even lower standard,

---

[148] Deer, B. (2004, February 22). *Revealed: MMR research scandal.* Thetimes.co.uk; The Times. https://www.thetimes.co.uk/article/revealed-mmr-research-scandal-7ncfntn8mjq

empathic thoughts about individuals who may refuse a vaccine, assuming you find vaccines desirable?

Did you take time to consider the varied causes, from general reticence about the state's heavy involvement in their development, sometimes with very strong personal conviction, to candidly held if also misinformed religious objections?

Did you consider that a person behaving according to misinformation may be better categorised as a victim than the village idiot, especially given that the British education system stopped teaching critical thinking in any formal way in 2005 (and thereby the most accurate way to evaluate information without needing another matrix by which to do it)?

Or did you simply do all but the mental equivalent of pointing, laughing, and then going about your day?

I am willing to bet any sum of money you like that the preponderance of you did the second; such behaviour seems a common trend in the modern day and I know I am guilty of it every day. The universality of ridicule as an approach is what creates this danger. This ridicule is also, ironically enough, self-defeating, if vaccine uptake rates are any indicator.

As already explored, the NHS is something of an institution above reproach with a lot of people in the UK. The pandemic, and the NHS idolatry[149] which has already been discussed and promoted by government, will no doubt make this even worse.

This is despite the NHS's sub-optimal handling of the virus as a whole, from its refusal to work with private firms at some early stages to save lives on account of nought but ideological bent, to concealing the promotion of that very ideology through the

---

[149] *Clap for our Carers every Thursday at 8pm #clapforourcarers.* (n.d.). Clap for Our Carers. Retrieved April 2, 2021, from: https://clapforourcarers.co.uk/

BBC.[150]

It has since emerged that, according to recently leaked data, COVID hospitalisations may have been hugely overblown in terms of infectivity in the general population, as the majority of COVID-labelled admissions only tested positive after being hospitalised.[151]

This of course doesn't mean that everyone who was hospitalised and tested positive after the fact had something other than COVID originally causing the problem, assuming that they either didn't take or lied about any previous test result.

But if one grants what seems the obvious assumption that hospitals should be treated differently to the wider environment for purposes of disease infectivity, then the fact that the majority of hospitalisations for COVID cannot decisively said to have happened outside those hospitals, at least as the data is presently constituted, is both condemnation of the hospitals and how the public has been lied to in pursuit of Project Fear.

The question of mandatory vaccination, which would in any other context arguably constitute state-sponsored wounding, assault by penetration and/or GBH, has been openly discussed.

This is because, for the purposes of UK law, wounding is treated interchangeably with GBH for the purposes of prosecution

[150] Singh, A. (2020, April 29). BBC defends Panorama show that used Labour activists to criticise lack of PPE. *The Telegraph.* https://www.telegraph.co.uk/news/2020/04/29/bbc-defends-panorama-show-used-labour-activists-criticise-lack/

[151] Donnelly, L., & Yorke, H. (2021, July 27). Exclusive: Over half of Covid hospitalisations tested positive after admission. The Telegraph. https://www.telegraph.co.uk/news/2021/07/26/exclusive-half-covid-hospitalisations-tested-positive-admission/?utm_content=telegraph&utm_medium=Social&utm_campaign=Echobox&utm_source=Facebook&fbclid=IwAR0rG2Jz2qsq7Fnx_YhEAhdzUBj_llmRnu4NDHteDW-N5RNpGg_CQI_5j5s#Echobox=1627343250-1

pursuant to Sections 18 and 20 of the Offences Against the Person Act 1861, and wounding is defined as any breach in the continuity of both the dermis and epidermis of the skin by the case of *C (A minor) v Eisenhower.*[152]

This analysis leaves aside the margin of appreciation and the disturbing European precedent of the state being allowed to compel citizens to accept medical treatments (seen at Paragraph 36 of the Judgment of *Solomakhin v Ukraine* in the European Court of Human Rights),[153] but stands for the point that mandatory vaccination would violate your bodily autonomy, one of your most fundamental rights, and set a precedent for its continued violation thereafter.

Furthermore, it was discussed in an openly and unfairly discriminatory manner—the suggestion was that NHS staff who refused a vaccine could or should be redeployed,[154] until unions stepped in with mitigating measures.[155]

There are other problems beside this.

Scepticism of the state, just as with everything else, is healthy. This has been a 'problem' when vaccinating minority communities—those whose ancestors were victimised by the state treat it with reticence for good reason and as such are, per capita,

---

[152] *ICLR.* (n.d.). Www.iclr.co.uk. Retrieved April 2, 2021, from https://www.iclr.co.uk/ic/1981000691

[153] Solomakhin v Ukraine, (ECHR March 15, 2012). http://health-rights.org/index.php/cop/item/case-of-solomakhin-v-ukraine

[154] Groves, J. (2021, March 2). *NHS staff could be forced to have COVID jab under new plans.* Mail Online. https://www.dailymail.co.uk/news/article-9318345/NHS-staff-forced-Covid-jab-radical-plans-reviewed-ministers.html

[155] Roberts, J. (2021, March 16). *NHS workers who refuse Covid vaccine could be redeployed.* Metro. https://metro.co.uk/2021/03/16/nhs-workers-who-refuse-covid-vaccine-could-be-redeployed-14251343/

less likely to take vaccines when offered.

Some may attempt to crowbar this scepticism into proving 'systemic racism', as discussed in this article, rather than allowing for the now-unfashionable idea (at least on the 'woke' left) that people can validly come to conclusions other than the party line.[156]

Many people hold religious concerns, perhaps unfounded but extant, nonetheless.

All factual information from this paragraph is drawn either from the previously footnoted Independent article, or the UK government's website, this area is particularly sensitive with good reason and so I wish to make this point as clinically as possible. You can find these facts at the website: gov.uk.[157]

Gelatine is used as a stabiliser in some vaccines. This helps them remain safe and effective during storage and transit. Three of the 'standard' vaccines given in the UK use it, which could be, though not necessarily depending on one's piety, problematic if you just so happen to be one of the 1.3 billion Muslims around the world.

There are readily available market alternatives which do not use gelatine of course and which would therefore bypass these religious concerns, but this part of the message isn't going to get across 100% of the time. Indeed, epistemic understanding might lead one to assert that no message which cannot be understood on a purely instinctive level ever will.

It is worth stating here that the UK's director of the Race and

---

[156] Lovett, S. (2021, March 29). *Vaccination rates continuing to lag among ethnic minority groups, new figures show.* The Independent. https://www.independent.co.uk/news/health/covid-vaccine-uptake-ethnicity-uk-b1823841.html

[157] *Vaccines and porcine gelatine.* (n.d.). GOV.UK. Retrieved April 2, 2021, from:
https://www.gov.uk/government/publications/vaccines-and-porcine-gelatine/vaccines-and-porcine-gelatine

Health Observatory has stated the following on the COVID vaccines specifically as also quoted in the article:

> *We need to be clear to our communities that there is no meat or meat products in the vaccine... There is no pork, there is no alcohol and it has been endorsed by religious leaders and religious councils.*

Again, the problem is not that the COVID vaccines themselves specifically have this issue in actuality, or that there aren't alternatives—there are.

The problem is conveying this information into what can often be insular communities. The point of view that the unvaccinated should be ridiculed then becomes hypocritical when one decides that any criticism of a decision against vaccination is worthy of censorship because of perceived absurdity or public health risk, only to then turn around and say that some intersection of the very groups who happen to fall into that category should be exempted from individual responsibility because of past wrongs committed against them and also that any such criticism is equivalent to bigotry, as the modern left increasingly demands. These vaccines are desirable, but their uptake must be voluntary and it is imperative that they not become another political football for authoritarians or point of cultural myopia, as seems rapidly to be happening.

The fundament of the point stands as follows: watch my image obsessed generation, especially the vapid 'woke' identitarians amongst them suddenly stop laughing when you point out that their fashionable punching down on this new *Untermensch* could manifest as, by their own standard, part of the Islamophobia they so enjoy lecturing everybody else about.

Their expressions will be priceless, I assure you. Aside from how enjoyable that may be, let us not engage in the very same ridicule that drives the vaccine hesitant away. It seems here that the best we can do is point out the manifest inconsistencies and hope that their presence is enough to inspire change. Failing that, continue to mobilise on your own terms.

This previous section was finished until very recently. This was before Boris Johnson decided to, once again, go back on his word about vaccine passports.

As before, his own government had promised in January of 2021 that they were not to be used, from his own vaccines minister no less.

However, when young people decided to exercise their human rights in a way not conducive to Johnson's agenda, he decided that the truth of his own government's word and the human right to bodily autonomy of 3 million people could be ran over by his ego.

First, it was put forward that those without double vaccination could not go to nightclubs—no great loss.

Then that they could not attend Premier League matches. Again, no great loss. Finally, that they could not attend university in person, after already having one, if not nearly two, years of their university experience robbed from them by the policies of his government.

He called this blackmail 'incentives.'

Let us be clear, a vaccine can be constituted as a violation of bodily autonomy because it must breach the skin and create a wound in order to be delivered, as prior the *JCC* definition given.

It is also the current and righteous consensus that, in order for consent to be valid, it must not be coerced in any way.

That is to say, if a man were to have sex with a woman whilst coercing her under the condition that she do it or she be subject to the removal of privilege or utility, and she would not have voluntarily consented, he would rightfully be called a rapist.

We cannot honestly expand from there and argue in full that the Johnson Ministry has engaged in a conspiracy to rape 3 million and has directed the actual rape of some figure of that 3 million; this is due to some peculiarities in English law that rape be committed with a penis and that it be sexual in nature.

Neither of those qualities apply to vaccines.

Vaccines also lack the intimate, visceral vulnerability that the topic of sexual violence does, hence the valid difference in tone with which the two are discussed. However, as consent is constituted at pure logic, aside from any entirely valid difference in feeling between the two incidents, the Johnson Ministry, and all NHS actuaries who have dispensed these coerced vaccines, have shown exactly the same coercive control and disregard for consent in favour of their desired outcome, exactly the same *mens rea*, that a criminal so charged would have shown.

I mention those NHS Actuaries to pre-empt the 'I was just following orders' non-defence.

Ultimately, the Johnson Ministry's words would remain exactly and only that if they did not have people willing to act upon them; so some aspect of guilt must be assigned to those who complied and carried out its will. I will conclude with this. There are 15 signs given that you may be in an abusive relationship by the Workplace Mental Health Institute.[158]

They are:

1. Stopping you from seeing friends and famiy
2. Stopping you from going outside without permission
3. Telling you what to wear

---

[158] Diaz, P. (n.d.). *Workplace Mental Health Resilience and Wellbeing Strategy in Australia, UK, USA.* https://www.thewmhi.com/. Retrieved July 28, 2021, from: https://www.thewmhi.com/

4. Monitoring your phone or emails
5. Controlling your finances or stopping you from working
6. Controlling information which you consume or produce
7. Constant monitoring
8. Punish you for breaking rules which constantly change
9. Telling you that this is for your own good and they know better
10. Not allowing you to question what is happening
11. Impressing to you that if you disagree, you are the only one and nobody agrees with you
12. Name-calling, belittling
13. Gaslighting
14. Dismissal of your opinion
15. Playing the victim

Now, go through that list, and see how many of those traits define your relationship with government generally, and/or the Johnson Ministry specifically.

I personally make 11/15 with the Johnson Ministry specifically, and with the many incarnations of statism, all 15 easily, but your sum may vary.

Exact matches are not the point being driven at, the next question to ask yourself is 'How many of these would you tolerate in a romantic partner?' If it is less than the amount which characterises your relationship with government and the Johnson Ministry, and you have not taken action to remove it from power, my next question, knowing that this pattern will continue unless stopped, is, 'How can you live with yourself?'

As before, conceptual discussion may lack the viscerality of topics and phenomena which are immediately and sensually obvious. It is all the more important therefore, that you summon up in yourself equivalent zeal to match the conceptual discussion to that which would be present if the violations discussed were happening right before your eyes. More important because, its not just you or I concerned.

It's everyone, now and the defenseless in the future, who are the victims of these predatory policies and behaviours, unless you give your all to stop it.

It matters not at this stage in terms of confirming the moral worth of the Johnson Ministry if these policies are passed into law, which they likely will be without further significant intervention. The mere open discussion confirms the fact that everyone in it, without exception, either actively retains the mindset of an abuser, or is willing to collaborate and collude with people who retain such a mindset and would take actions pursuant to it (actions which also violate any internally coherent view of law and human rights) in order to enact a broader shared goal. Which leads us nicely onto the actions which must be taken on this basis...

Current Conclusions and Further Actions

Much has changed in the theatre of British politics over the time it took to write this chapter.

Advisors have been expended and replaced, news platforms have roared and flopped, and the *zeitgeist* of the nation has lurched from lockdown-craving, to marching in the streets when politically and emotionally convenient, and back to self-flagellation.

One theme has remained absolutely constant: the utter incompetence and hypocrisy of the First Johnson Ministry, combined with the ineffectuality of its opposition.

I mentioned that we would further consider that hypocrisy earlier; it was recently pointed out to me that some particularly twisted in their thinking might regard the ability to preach hypocrisy without consequence as an emblem and endorsement of social power. The ability to so nakedly parade contradicting statements and behaviours before the public to no punishment, and at times rising public support, might in some deluded minds represent ego's conquest of truth.

The solipsists would have infiltrated 'Conservatism', an impressive feat.

To all who value consistent ethics and the open presentation of whatever one regards to be objective truth, this would seem to be an aberration.

So, what is to be done?

The first answer is to accept the most difficult premise—no party in the UK Parliament is a friend to policies which could even be called classically liberal, never mind libertarian or voluntarist.

There may be individual members of those parties who are so inclined, and who do valuable work that should not be denigrated unnecessarily.

However, the incentives at play of continually pumping more money into the public purse and, let us not forget, continuing to heap more debt onto the shoulders of non-consenting children are overwhelming for those with designs on *imperium*.

So, it is now clear that there must be a new political enterprise.

This, despite the political landscape of recent years being littered with stillborn new parties. For what it's worth, Philip Davies MP confirmed to me that the prospect of a cross-party coalition of members drawn from the current parties looking to defend liberty, at least as negatively conceived, is not viable.

The Independent Group, short-lived as it was, should be an example of such a failure.

We must therefore mobilise to demonstrate proof-of-concept for such a movement at the grassroots level before expecting any chance of success at upper political strata.

Organisations such as Momentum, loathe though we may be to admit it, have proven very effective in such endeavours.

Parallels in defense of liberty must be organised, mobilised, and set forth to that effect.

Further, a key and clear distinction must be maintained from the goliaths of Parliament, this to avoid subsumption. A consistent ethical stance must be both promulgated and demanded to base that identity on, and the Parliamentary parties abandonment of such clarity must be hammered home with every opportunity.

This enterprise must be carried onwards through every avenue possible. The UK has greater potential for the restoration of liberty than elsewhere, on account of the greater power of the legislative and executive than elsewhere—if secured, liberty could be reconstituted far more quickly and far more totally than in other jurisdictions.

But by the very same token, the same is true for those who wish to destroy it.

It is for this reason that this new enterprise is necessary, to maintain vigilance at the least and to aim for far greater goals.

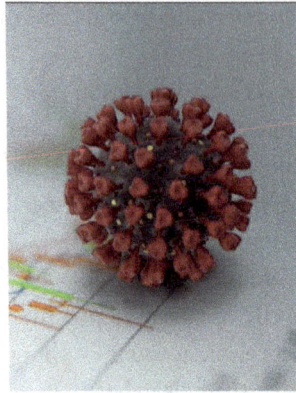

Chapter 6—Asia and Australasia, as Liberty sets in the West, a new Brand Rises in the East

To receive a favour is to sell one's liberty.
—Japanese Proverb

I discovered freedom for the first time in England
—Hirohito

The Outlook on COVID in Japan

A NATION SITTING similarly in output, if not philosophy, to the Swedish approach to handling COVID-19, was Japan.

There are many different reasons given by many different advocates for Japan's good management of the crisis: the government response, a milder strain of the virus, cultural habits, and other behaviours such as higher rates of wearing face masks, along with more regular hand washing with sanitizing equipment, a protective genetic trait, and a relative immunity conferred by the mandatory BCG tuberculosis vaccine.

That last part is especially disturbing for deontological lovers of liberty; we discussed in chapters prior how the idea of a mandatory vaccination is horrifying for people who value bodily autonomy and sanctity from state incursion.

However, given the exemplary speed with which the Japanese dealt with the virus, one feels it necessary to discuss their method.

Better our side be known as and when governments look for other examples they can follow when the next pandemic strikes, than omit it because some facts in the scenario cut both ways.

Therefore, let us now move to examine each point of differentiation, and look for exactly how relevant it is.

Japan is not the only example of interesting examples in the Eastern Hemisphere—the New Zealander's response was unilaterally praised in the UK and the different approach taken by the Australians is also worthy of discussion.

China remains of course, the elephant in the room, with the WHO taking a fresh interest in the origins of the virus in that country. India was often contrasted to New Zealand – images from that country of COVID-induced fungus infections were one of the things used to terrify my own countrymen into submission.

However let us begin with discussion of Japan, before moving elsewhere.

A More Competent Government?

The first state of emergency declared by the Japanese government was, incredibly short by other standards. It lasted less than two months, from decree on April 7th of 2020 to its setting down on the 25th of May across the entire country. There was, admittedly a second, declared on the 7th of January 2021 for several prefectures and lasting until the 22nd of March.

However, lockdowns, such as we would conceive of them, did not exist in Japan for any lengthy period of time, and were deployed with great reticence even within states of emergency. For those wishing to analyse freedom consequentially, the Japanese approach to COVID-19 stands out as a shining exemplar.

I hope I have already made clear however, why I think deontological analyses of liberty must always reign supreme.

So perhaps the instinctive response is that the Japanese example stands as a counterargument to the prior worries about government abuse?

Perhaps governments which grant themselves near total power can be sufficiently motivated by civic duty to self-regulate, just as voluntarists might argue a company or labour union in possession of any surplus power over its own market would out of desire to discipline itself before being disciplined by those it would antagonise.

Even granting the theoretical or practical instance of this (it would be difficult to tell in any case whether the government in question was truly beneficent, or just much better at hiding its corrupt tendencies) we again default to probabilistic analysis.

Which is more likely to abuse a surplus of power, and which can do so to a greater or more total effect?

Multiply the values and you have a basic index to show you which is riskier—construct that index however you wish, I will not suggest one here. It seems a viable initial suggestion that the calculus will not come out in the statists favour.

There has come about an unfortunate discussion based on the idea of differing national cultures, in terms of unique elements and qualities.

Such discussion is often full of unfortunate invective, pride and mysticism which muddies the waters of what information is actually pertinent and what can be usefully discussed. The discussion most clearly came about, or seems to have done so, as a result of comments by the Japanese Deputy Prime Minister Taro Aso.

The comment was reported in the BBC as follows:[159]

> *I told these people: 'Between your country and our country, mindo (the level of people [or cultural level]) is different.' And that made them speechless and quiet.*

Social and hard scientists alike tend to, in my experience, despise any proposed solution or aspect of a solution which depends on cultural uniqueness. This is understandable and seems to me a very valid objection. It is difficult enough to isolate and compare culture in one instance by its very nature, never mind retroactively project and model back to where it was first incepted along with any unique elements and in turn how and why those elements became a part of the culture in question.

This is part of the reason why ideas such as the Protestant Work Ethic are maligned today as unscientific and little more than self-aggrandisation on account of authors infected with delusions of cultural superiority.[160]

Assume that distinct cultures each have distinct elements, as this argument would require. Assume that each of these distinct elements may create an advantage towards stated ends under certain circumstances and a disadvantage under others.

Ceteris paribus, there might be a degree of difficulty in

---

[159] Wingfield-Hayes, R. (2020, July 3). *Coronavirus: Japan's mysteriously low virus death rate.* BBC.
https://www.bbc.com/news/amp/world-asia-53188847
[160] Fernand Braudel. (1990). *Afterthoughts on material civilization and capitalism.* Johns Hopkins University Press.

transplanting these unique elements from culture to culture as they may be, and in some cases are, contextually dependent. As such there may be limited point in their discussion beyond what can be accurately and rationally digested, courtesy of the bounds imposed on human rationality by the corresponding condition.

This would stand in normal circumstances, never even mind those where special attention is being cast on a given characteristic which is thought to be relevant to an immediately present flashpoint, with a lack of consideration as to its other facets. If not, there would be nothing unique to comment on in the first place, and no distinction between different cultures, which seems an absurd conclusion, at least assuming that there is sufficient interchange between cultures, by whatever means, for any absolutely advantageous traits to outcompete disadvantageous ones.

I am not a sociologist by trade, and there are doubtless resources out there where one could learn that practice better. But I hope I have here encapsulated the scientific objection, or at least my understanding of it, here. Even if it is true, which is not proven, that cultures can develop advantageous traits in and of themselves by force of circumstance, then the locally understood nature of that trait would prevent its exportation, digestion and understanding by most scientific methods which depend upon the abstraction and comparison of the knowledge in question against a given universal standard or test.

The far better explanation seems to be that we have observed here a simple policy difference. This may have contributed to the increased effectiveness, at least in consequential terms, to the Japanese response to COVID-19.

But it would be incorrect to attempt to extrapolate an entire cultural difference out of it, or to make it fit into some unscientific theme of cultural uniqueness against probabilistically superior and preferably simpler explanations.

A Milder Strain?

This argument seems to be at least scientifically more appealing than the previous in and of itself.

Keyword, 'seems.'

I say this because it suffers from a similar paucity of evidence, or at least seems to at this time. Some outlets, such as Cambridge News, have reported of new and differing outbreaks in Japan. But even where this is the case, they do not assert that the strain in question is milder, on the contrary, that 'it may be more contagious than domestic variants.'

One of the better sources I could find was a commentary by EMBO Molecular Medicine.[161]

It stated the following on the 'milder strain' hypothesis:

> *While possible, there is no current evidence that milder strains of SARS-CoV-2 exist. Nor do we know what sort of antibody response would develop as a result of exposure to such a hypothetical variant. Phylogenetic analysis of SARS-CoV-2 of more than 3,500 SARS-CoV-2 genomes from around the world, including 29 from Japan, suggests that the outbreak in Japan was sparked by several independent virus introductions primarily from China ... (Hadfield et al, 2018). Furthermore, all of the SARS-CoV-2 genomes are highly similar; most contain no more than 10 mutations compared to the virus that started the original outbreak. Thus, it is highly unlikely that*

---

[161] Iwasaki, A., & Grubaugh, N. D. (2020). *Why does Japan have so few cases of COVID-19?* EMBO Molecular Medicine, *12(5)*. https://doi.org/10.15252/emmm.202012481

> *the virus has evolved a significantly different*
> *phenotype, and even less likely that it was*
> *introduced early into Japan*

We could end this section there, but if true, some parts of that quoted section seem to have important broader implications.

This seems to put a dent in the worries of people going on about different vaccines being needed to combat every different strain. Over 3,500 different genomes could not possibly each be covered by 3,500 types of vaccine.

But the blade cuts both ways.

This would also eliminate the demands for unlimited social distancing and other measures until all variants have been dealt with or rendered into non-issues by herd immunity, at least assuming you want a functional economy to come back to afterwards.

If there is no known antibody differential in exposure to different strains, at least based on severity, then it is pointless to continue these morally bankrupt and economically suicidal policies waiting for a biological phenomenon which would never happen.

Cultural Habits and Face Masks

EMBO also discuss this point:

> *It is certainly true that the Japanese customs do not*
> *involve handshaking, hugging, or kissing when*
> *greeting. In addition, many Japanese [people] wear*
> *cloth or paper face masks (not the N95 respirators*
> *required for exclusion of aerosol viral particles) in*
> *the winter to avoid transmission of respiratory*
> *infections. People use the mask to avoid spreading*
> *the infection and also in an attempt to prevent*

exposure to infection.

However, we are unconvinced that this is the main or only reason why COVID-19 is so well contained in Japan. There is no social distancing in rush hour trains and buses, or when walking in crowded streets to school or to work. The use of face mask is also practiced in other Asian countries that witnessed higher rates of infection. A hint to whether this is a valid hypothesis comes from looking at other pandemic viral respiratory diseases. The community R0 rate for the 2009 pandemic flu for Japan was 1.28 while USA was 1.7–2.0 (Boelle et al, 2011). Thus, R0 in Japan was somewhat lower than the global median R0 of 1.47. In addition, an observational study of elementary school children in Japan found that wearing masks had significant protective association (odds ratio of 0.859, 95% confidence interval 0.778–0.949) against seasonal influenza (Uchida et al, 2017). Therefore, the social practice culture of Japan and mask use may explain to some extent the lower number of observed COVID-19 cases but is unlikely the only explanation.

It seems EMBO hammer on one of the points I've been driving at in this section, but it bears elaboration and anticipation of development.

It will be difficult, both now and moving onwards to separate different causes from one another when explaining differentials in severity, infectivity and so on.

It is also worth considering another rationalisation those who point to cultural differences might engage in—they may accept the prior elimination of any deductively provable cultural difference in influencing such phenomena, but may argue that one could inductively identify certain attributes, lump them together with the trepidation one must take in such fields of study given confidence thresholds and the lack of ironclad guarantees, and call that chimera a cultural difference.

For example, I speculate that some thinking along the lines of and wishing to defend the thinking of Deputy Prime Minister Aso might concede the point that behaviours like those EMBO identify need not be deductively unique to Japanese society.

They might argue that the observation of their presence at the pertinent point in time combined with observations like the lower community R0 rate priorly observed is sufficient evidence to induce a remarkable cultural difference, dispensing with the need to demand and analyse any prior continuity of history.

The last clause points to the refutation—if cultures become by this logic, creatures which can be exhaustively described by a single inductive sample at a convenient point in time (any alternative demands some sampling of continuous history and thereby either an expansion of the inductive method to a point uncomfortably subject to Xeno's Paradox, or a default back to a deductive measure), all uniqueness asserted by those making the very argument collapses.

All which would have to happen would be for the perceived 'others' to copy the remarked upon characteristics, and the cultural differences in question would cease to exist. The response I anticipate in such a circumstance would be that this response is one of admission or surrender—we would be cutting off our nose to spite our face by arguing against significant cultural differences whilst transplanting what the opposition would claim to be exactly those differences, presumably for some perceived or actual benefit in the process.

In which case we would default back to the initial refutation, slightly elaborated, alongside the note that observing the possibility of transplanting cultural ideas does not lock that in as the only course of action. Cultures, as typically conceived by nationalists, patriots and other groupthinkers, though I hasten to add not necessarily implied from anything Minister Aso has being quoted as saying here, tend not to simply be, at least in their mind, describable as a series of points in a given answer space which happen to be interlinked at any one time.

Such creatures of circumstance could, theoretically, given enough possible universes and possibilities, be perfectly replicated and therefore, would not be unique, at least by the semantic meaning of the term. There is almost always, in the groupthinker's view, some assertion of either inherent or earned uniqueness.

This is normally granted by one of two ways.

The first is by the vicissitudes of some magisterium so conveniently separated as to be non-falsifiable or held to be so by those claiming its non-falsifiability. For examples, see every theocracy and arguably every religion-referencing state across history, but also imperialist 'civilising missions.'

The other is that of a right earned by virtue of some prior experience or sunk cost which is uniquely understood by their collective experience of the hugely improbable permutation of events which occurred across multiple points in time, see 'manifest destiny' and the various claimants to the successorship of the Roman Empire across European and Middle Eastern history.

The fundament of the refutation is that those arguing for cultural uniqueness as an asset against COVID cannot have it both ways—they cannot have transplantable, identifiable and definite assets which influence the core biology at play, as well as some mysterious and indecipherable legacy which sets them aside from all others.

There may be some cultures which are not advocated for with that uniqueness, which would flaw the refutation in their case, but if they are extant then they are outside the author's limited knowledge. We can therefore cast this argument aside with no further discussion.

Protected by Genetics?

This explanation must be considered carefully, especially so when placed into the context of prior the immediately prior discussions.

Differences in susceptibility to infection based on genetics are handily explained, at least in theory, here.[162]

The article itself makes very clear that it reports on information that is not yet peer-reviewed and as such is not yet entrenched. However, preliminary studies discussed therein seem to indicate that COVID-19, or susceptibility thereto, is influenced by certain genetic factors. It follows that this may help explain the different reactions to the virus between individuals.

This produces another layer of variation in addition to all the 'strains' of COVID-19 commonly discussed in the media.

Other studies have examined susceptibility to COVID-19 and genetic variation thereon on the chromosomal level.[163]

One key point from this study is that these chromosomal differences vary by geography—to quote the article:

> *The study also reveals considerable differences in how common this genetic risk variant is in different parts of the world. It is particularly common among people in South Asia where about half of the*

---

[162] *Common genetic variants may influence susceptibility to COVID-19.* (2020, September 23). News-Medical.net. https://www.news-medical.net/news/20200923/Common-genetic-variants-may-influence-susceptibility-to-COVID-19.aspx

[163] Zeberg, H., & Pääbo, S. (2020, September 30). *Neandertal gene variant increases risk of severe Covid-19.* Www.mpg.de. https://www.mpg.de/15451493/neandertal-genes-covid19

population carry the Neandertal risk variant. In Europe, one in six people carry the risk variant, while in Africa and East Asia it is almost non-existent.

Whilst the study in question was not able to explain exactly why this chromosomal difference exists, but it should not be disregarded as a potential explanation as to why the situation was far worse in Europe than Japan and far worse in South Asia than Europe in turn, though of course, other differentials exist. This seems to be especially true in serious cases of COVID-19 requiring ventilation:

> *Today, the people who inherited this gene variant are three times more likely to need artificial ventilation if they are infected by the novel coronavirus SARS-CoV-2.*

It would seem then, looking forward to the future, that some mechanism to test for this gene variant and alert people to its existence may be helpful. Both to inform people as to the likely needs of their own healthcare, and for prioritisation of treatment and vaccination along consequential terms, where such prioritisation is morally acceptable. Usual caveats and trepidation applies, but on my cursory survey, this explanation seems to hold some promise.

The BCG Vaccine and Imported Immunity?

EMBO had this to say to on the idea of the BCG vaccine importing immunity, or relative immunity, to COVID-19:

> *Japan, like many other countries including China,*

George Beglan

Korea, India, and the Russian Federation have mandatory childhood BCG vaccines against tuberculosis. These countries have so far a relatively low per capita death rate from COVID-19 compared to countries that have no mandatory BCG vaccines (USA, Spain, France, Italy, The Netherlands). What further distinguishes Japan is that the BCG vaccine strain used in Japan, Brazil, and Russia is one of the original strains, while further modified BCG strains are used for vaccination in European countries. This association between BCG vaccination and apparent low COVID-19 incidence in Japan has spurred the idea that these two things may be linked...

How would BCG, an attenuated bacterial vaccine completely unrelated to COVID-19, provide protection? Michai Netea and colleagues hypothesized that the vaccine may boost "trained immunity" (Netea et al, 2016) ... Studies have shown that receipt of BCG vaccine was associated with a reduction in all-cause mortality within the first 1– 60 months: The average relative risks were 0.70 (95% confidence interval 0.49–1.01) from five clinical trials (Higgins et al, 2016)...

I need not further emphasise or preach further on the nonviability of mandatory vaccination as an offence against any deontological construction of liberty.

This despite multiple nations and authorities sneaking it into law in the case of COVID by leveraging access to society against the consent of those who otherwise would not. Many other nations have mandatory vaccinations against other diseases either in place for children or as a condition of access for many other things.

Promotion of trained immunity from a young age as a method for reducing mortalities across the board seems a relatively favourable dystopia in the case that thoughts like those conveyed in *Solomakhin* become reflected in laws around the world.

Further, any potential synergies between vaccines for the immune system might constitute a good way of increasing uptake—if some are reticent about receiving a COVID vaccine on account of a seemingly suspicious rapidity of development then pointing to effects it would have against other diseases may be a good way of tying it back into the wider picture of public health in people's minds.

The inverse may also apply for how other vaccines and building a wider portfolio of health in one's own life help combat COVID.

The technocrats and their cultists seem to have, luckily for the rest of us, created their own marketing problem in this regard. By offering themselves and their policies of grinding liberty to rendered meat under false security's treads as a total solution to a problem which has so thoroughly dominated people's lives, any other competing solutions become unattractive as far as they cannot be incorporated into that vision.

This will probably be easy enough to solve as a branding issue; people can be reminded of health services and how they help build a health profile; to be keep all vaccines up to date and so on.

What must be emphasised then, for their absorption of this to be denied to any degree, is the individual agency in those choices; the ability to mobilise it to protect one's health and autonomy must be promulgated above all else.

Conclusions on Japan

Drawing the threads of the first part of this section together may seem to be an exercise of counting the nails that have been hammered at throughout. That scientifically, it will be difficult to separate individual conditions from each other as far as they interact with COVID-19's infectivity, severity and lethality and that according measures must be added into our arguments.

Philosophically, whilst the Japanese approach ranks the same deontologically at least with regards to liberty as the other statist approaches taken around the globe, it may at least be saved by some motivation of civic duty.

When analysed consequentially, it has been far more effective than those taken in other democracies and, if one is purely analysing by this matrix, there would be lessons to be learned and measures to be copied. However, even this may be unsafe as an assumption—there is no way to guarantee that compliance rates are universal across instances of the same place, never mind different places, and so what works in one place may not retain the same effectiveness elsewhere.

What then, is to be taken away from the discussion?

First of all, readiness against those who would use the example to point to consequential justifications to infringe liberty, in that ultimately the vast majority of measures aim towards the same goal and the dichotomy between the two approaches remains no matter the strengths a given set of policies had or has.

Secondly and downstream from the first, to clarify the criteria on which this debate should take place. It should well be, but regrettably seems not to be, a statement of the obvious that COVID-19 as a phenomenon and the disastrous policies surrounding its emergence should not be a scapegoat for any re-emergence or promotion of groupthink, unjust generalisation or populism.

Yet that it quite clearly has been, in Japan and all over the world, and sometimes with far more severe consequences.

The many ideas and conceptualisations of unique cultures must be carefully distinguished—the ugly idea that such separation is derivable on account of some inherent characteristic about the people concerned, rather than the collective weight of decisions made by, for and to them does not logically stand, but merely pointing this out is clearly not enough to defeat this fallacious narrative.

The effort of removing it from consciousness and towards individuality in thought on every level would be outside the remit of this book and require volumes multiples of its length to fully encompass.

However, by the very same stroke, disregarding inductive observations about how different cultures have affected their handling of COVID and how they value freedom alongside other rights would cut against much of what this book has itself already discussed.

It remains true, that whilst observations on this approach remain valuable, the caveats must be stated—observation of differences in circumstance must be treated clinically and not hijacked to resurrect some other ulterior political purpose.

Australia and New Zealand— Twinned by Geography, Divergent in Policy

To us, health is about so much more than simply not being sick. It's about getting a balance between physical, mental, emotional, cultural and spiritual health. Health and healing are interwoven, which means that one can't be separated from the other.
—Dr. Tamara Mackean

Endemic Mitigation in Australia—and How Destroying Liberty Does Not Produced The Advertised Results

We'll begin first with Australia.

The nation's approach began with the controversial goal of 'suppression' as opposed to 'elimination' of COVID-19. The Australian response may not have been raised to the outright idyllic standard that Ardern's New Zealand has been, but it has, despite the expectation that new outbreaks will occur, been viewed relatively favourably alongside its counterparties, though less so given the slower rate of its vaccine rollout.

It would seem at the outset then that a realist's view trumps one which is overly ambitious. Some might even go so far as to suggest that the Australians saw the endemic nature of COVID-19, rather than just some temporary pandemic, long before others. There's also another factor to bear in mind—some may remember the tragically wide bushfires which raged through much of Australia just prior to the international outbreak of COVID-19 as 2019 became 2020.

These fires in turn resulted in much decreased volume of tourists for Australia in that year, which may have substantially reduced infections in the early stages of the pandemic outside of any policy decision.[164]

Moreover, there were certain key differences between the Australian approach and those taken in the U.S. and in Western Europe. These included an earlier imposition of travel restrictions to minimize infections from the world over, a very successful

---

[164] Long, Q. (n.d.). *Australia dodged a COVID-bullet via the Summer Bushfires*. News.com.Au. Retrieved July 19, 2021, from:
https://www.news.com.au/national/australia-dodged-a-covidbullet-via-the-summer-bushfires/video/fe16d8b39d583bb13e9e8440470e7bed

182

recruitment of tracing workforce and intense lockdowns which were used to exhaustively model out sources of infectivity rather than as general preventative measures.

All this came together with a considerably greater degree of public trust to create a model which worked well for achieving its stated ends.

As ever, the technocrats were unhappy with any aim which did not immediately hand them power on a silver platter and imperfect their coup d' grace. Criticisms were therefore mounted, that the approach was cynical, cold and fatalistic. Or, did the Australian approach simply accepted the inevitable and act accordingly?

A comparison which it provided to the UK and elsewhere— how different administrations exploited COVID-19 to set up state surveillance apparatus under cover of public health.

Let us take a brief detour back to the UK and its NHS app to have something to compare against.

Owned and operated by the NHS, able to trace and reconstruct where you have been, and containing the vaccination status of whoever has it which is: 'Only accessible [by you] from the app.'

It's bad enough that state parties are being trusted with this kind of information blindly by people, the same way they trust social media companies with it. Figures vary on the number of people who installed it, and even then those who used it 'correctly.'

After it identified a series of ministers who needed to self-isolate, who initially attempted to circumvent that requirement of their own law with a pilot scheme they had declined to inform the nation about before that point, it was suggested that its sensitivity might need to be adjusted.

Convenient timing…

Reports of it 'pinging' people through walls between establishments and pinging people in a legally actionable way

George Beglan

without even notifying them abounded.[165] This is already compounding the NHS's record on protecting the cybersecurity of the people it is supposed to care for; that record has been blotched by the 2017 mass cyberattack[166] in which it was discovered that the Service was lazily and knowingly using out of date operating systems, only acting once any damage had already been done. In short, the NHS record on cybersecurity is lacklustre at best and their own app certainly isn't optimised for healthcare.

I submit that this is because it was not built with healthcare in mind, at least in the sense of direct provision; it was built as a surveillance apparatus which was then co-opted into a healthcare purpose.

It has not been NHS policy to admit people to hospital with COVID-19 in every instance—this is one of the few things which makes sense as such measures would be patently unnecessary. The approach has instead been one of prevention, this is the point of self-isolation and tracking people.

However, though any invasion of privacy is to voluntarists and most young people active online disgusting, consider a halfway house approach which could have been developed. Consider a one-way system which let people know that they might be at risk by holding the reconstruction data with a third party charged with keeping it secure under trust or deleting it after notifying all who needed to be.

Open Data Institute research, funded by the UK government,

---

[165] Elgot, J. (2021, August 2). *Ministers to update NHS Covid app to "reduce disruption."* The Guardian. https://www.theguardian.com/world/2021/aug/02/ministers-to-update-nhs-covid-app-to-reduce-disruption

[166] House of Commons Committee of Public Accounts. (2018). *Cyberattack on the NHS.* In Parliament.uk. https://publications.parliament.uk/pa/cm201719/cmselect/cmpubacc/787/787.pdf

outlined such a possibility with some slight redefinitions[167] and was discussed later at my own Oxford Law Faculty,[168] all prior to the development of this app.

To no avail apparently...

We could still be in a halfway house if it were to go so far as to keep that evidence locally stored on the host device without collecting this data and sending it back to the NHS and therefore the state for compilation.

At the very least, one which anonymised it by only providing a readout of total numbers at risk and similar statistics rather than locality and reconstruction data. If the NHS still wanted or needed that data, it could ask explicitly rather than stealthing it onto people's mobile phones, or Parliament, busied with new legislation, could have added the capacity to seize it should evidence be mustered under warrant.

Those who developed severe symptoms could have been instructed to bring themselves to hospital via the public broadcasts going on at the time and those who did not would know to self-isolate. Should they have failed to do so or been suspected of breaching the tyrannical Coronavirus Act, the appropriate prosecutors would immediately have the evidence to hand upon servicing a warrant on the device.

All that would be required would be for prosecutors to do their jobs and for the burden of proof to be upheld—that the maxim of innocent until proven guilty be maintained. Why not use

---

[167] *Huge appetite for data trusts, according to new ODI research*—The ODI. (2019, April 15). TheODI.org.
https://theodi.org/article/huge-appetite-for-data-trusts-according-to-new-odi-research/

[168] McFarlane, B. (2019). *Data Trusts and Defining Property.* Property Law Blog.
https://www.law.ox.ac.uk/research-and-subject-groups/property-law/blog/2019/10/data-trusts-and-defining-property

this system?

A system which would still constitute a massive invasion of privacy, even with this halfway house modification which do nothing but protect people's rights and demand that procedures already in place under the law be maintained, instead of throwing *habeus corpus* under the bus and handing police and prosecutors leverage they have so patently abused in who they chose to target and prey upon.

Why has this system, as far as I can tell from surveying the public consciousness, not even been considered?

Because those who built it never cared about your rights, and never will. Worse than that, they wanted to build a system which would turn each person against everyone else's rights, to create a culture of reporting people for breaching regulations and for busybodies to reign supreme.

One can inspect the adverts the government ran on YouTube for confirmation of this. 'Let's Not Go Back, join the millions already vaccinated.' is not a scientific argument as to the effectiveness or desirability of vaccines—despite the fact that a very compelling argument can be and is made. It's a veiled threat, that the government retains the power to take your life away again, followed by social blackmail.

As before, the technocrats don't want to debate the issue, they do not care about your opinion or you. It's been nonarguments first, then emotional blackmail and failing that, throwing rights and due process, or at least the principles behind them off a cliff.

However bad the UK was on this front, Australia was worse. So much so, that the Australian Government openly calls one of its action plans the: 'Australian National Disease Surveillance Plan for COVID-19' and openly advertises it for consumption by the general populace.[169]

Prior to this, the Inspector General of Intelligence and Security openly admitted that the country's security services had 'incidentally' collected data from the Australian version of the contact tracing app, COVIDSafe, from May to November of 2020.[170]

If the populace still care for their rights, public discontent of this is not noted anywhere in the discussion of it. Whether 'incidentally' means that the data was collected tangentially in the course of other operations, or case by case for independent processing and operation, it's hard to find another Anglospheric nation which has been so naked about its surveilling of its citizens and to such negligible reprisal.

I'm reminded of the Italian Blackshirt motto: 'Mi no frego.' Meaning: 'I don't give a damn'. It wasn't just a label, it was a mission statement—to condition the populace to the necessary predicates for their totalitarian vision not by brutal public repression and reminding people of the constant presence of the party, but by the inverse.

By turning the national attitude into one of apathy and as such, removing all opposition far more permanently. 50 years ago, similar scandals like Watergate, albeit that was far more deliberate and far reaching, toppled Presidencies in nations far more

---

[169] Australian Government Department of Health. (2020, May 29). *Australian National Disease Surveillance Plan for COVID-19.* Australian Government Department of Health.
https://www.health.gov.au/resources/publications/australian-national-disease-surveillance-plan-for-covid-19
[170] Inspector-General of Intelligence and Security. (16 C.E.). COVID app data and Intelligence Agencies within IGIS Jurisdiction. In *Documentcloud.org.*
https://www.documentcloud.org/documents/20416358-report-to-oaic-may-nov-2020-covidsafe-app#document/p2/a2005851

powerful, with interests one would think, far more determined.

But now, the statists and surveillers seemed to have succeeded in their objective—its not just that they, the perpetrators, don't care about the implications of such behaviour, they never have and never will—they have managed to create an environment in which citizens and people, the victims, do not care about their own rights either.

Surveillance and the destruction of privacy at the request of any unnamed government actuary has ceased to be scandal and has become, by the promulgation of apathy and the use of clever-sounding nonarguments like the classic: 'If you have nothing to fear, you have nothing to hide', an acceptable modus operandi of politics.

There's more to come, predictably so.

Proposed in 2014, there remain 7 years later several proposals under discussion which will no doubt be expedited in pursuit of the perfect COVID police state. These include giving the Australian Security Intelligence Organisation (ASIO) the right to hack into and modify computers, to spy on whole computer networks, and presumably any third party traffic which enters it, by a single warrant.

Still more, proposals also include giving the Australian Security Intelligence Service (ASIS) the ability to spy on Australians overseas, creating a blanket criminal charge punishable with 10 years in jail time for whistleblowing or revealing secret information, even if done unintentionally.

So long *mens rea*, it was nice knowing you.

Rounding out the next step towards Australian tyranny would be the mandatory retention of all telecommunications data for two years. These proposals should shock you—they should turn you away from investing in or dealing with any IT company based in or with any links to the Australian authorities concerned and they should serve as a warning. A warning that this is a model of what is to come.

If public apathy if continues, if those concerned fail to come together and demand a final, continually and permanently transparent end to such policies, you can wave goodbye to any privacy.

We can compare the final results of the Australian approach to others towards the end of the pandemic, or at least the stage where it morphs into an endemic, with a current case-fatality rate of 2.8% as of the time of writing, to be treated with the same scepticism as those gathered from elsewhere, according to Johns Hopkins. This is above the UK, at 2.2%, Spain at 1.9%, the United States at 1.8% and New Zealand at 0.9%, compare to others at your will.

Let the authoritarians answer this—per capita, lives were not saved by their policies. So why on Earth, should they be tolerated any longer? [171]

New Zealand and New Age Icons

The burning question, from those observing outside New Zealand, I wager is most probably—'Is the media praise justified?'

As of the time of writing, only 26 people have been confirmed to have died from COVID-19 in the country, yielding a case-fatality rate of a paltry 0.9%. It's not just that lethality is markedly lower in the country when compared to many of its peers, but also the amount of infections as a proportion of the population.

Only 2,865 cases have been confirmed or deemed as probable across the entire country as of the time of writing, or some 0.05%

---

[171] John Hopkins University. (2021). *Mortality Analyses.* Johns Hopkins Coronavirus Resource Center.
https://coronavirus.jhu.edu/data/mortality

of the total population.[172]

This, despite the fact that near 2 million tests had been carried out months before the time of writing, towards the end of March of 2021.[173]

So, if measures were to be successful, total infectivity might remain low, presuming the test figure against the confirmed infections is anywhere near accurate.

Of course, these tests might have been carried out once and at the wrong time with people being infected afterwards, so we must allow some margin for error, but this does not satisfactorily explain the huge differential observed between New Zealand and other states in terms of the proportion of the population infected.

The fact that this further strengthens the prior argument drawing on Pascal's Wager in that it would seem to indicate that COVID may not necessarily be endemic in certain circumstances, will of course be conveniently sidestepped by technocrats unless they are forced to address it.

Remarkable figures.

That's not to say that handling was flawless.

Public trust in the healthcare system and government in the country after its response, most encouragingly after the announcement of lockdowns.

There were anti-lockdown protests, regrettably corrupted by conspiracy theories and anti-vaxxers.

Debate is still ongoing as to the credibility of sources used by those involved, though the rebuttal from those protesting in reply to initial criticisms has yet to attract any attention, so the group is

---

[172] Ibid.

[173] *No new community cases; 8 cases of COVID-19 in managed isolation; 1 historical case.* (2021, March 22). Ministry of Health NZ. https://www.health.govt.nz/news-media/media-releases/no-new-community-cases-8-cases-covid-19-managed-isolation-1-historical-case

most likely forsaken in any relevance.

Its corresponding political party has already declared intent to deregister, so any further debate on it is likely to be an exercise in futility, irrespective of factual merit.

Other aspects will be criticised, like education sources being directed to reach out to 'appropriate sources' to teach as an attempt at censorship by control amongst others. Yet consequentially, the observation stands that New Zealand seems to have so far excelled her peers.

This observation stands in the case of the government and the people. Bloomberg's COVID-resilience rankings in late April of 2021 ranked New Zealand as the second best state in the world. Alastair Campbell, Tony Blair's spin doctor in chief, praised Arden[174] alongside The Washington Post.[175]

High praise indeed—the relative paucity of this section may stand out but, there is not much more remarkable or distinctive to say about New Zealand's government measures, at least from a bird's eye view.

Perhaps that very ordinality is the most compelling argument against further statist incursion from the statists' point of view— they need not make expensive political ventures if they can simply convince people to adhere to measures proven to work and relatively tame in scope.

---

[174] Campbell, A. (2020, April 11). *Alastair Campbell: Jacinda Ardern's coronavirus plan is working because unlike others, she's behaving like a true leader.* The Independent.
https://www.independent.co.uk/voices/coronavirus-new-zealand-jacinda-ardern-cases-deaths-leadership-a9460591.html
[175] Fifield, A. (2020, April 7). *New Zealand isn't just flattening the curve. It's squashing it.* The Washington Post.
https://www.washingtonpost.com/world/asia_pacific/new-zealand-isnt-just-flattening-the-curve-its-squashing-it/2020/04/07/6cab3a4a-7822-11ea-a311-adb1344719a9_story.html

A sub-optimal concession, but also a good litmus test to sort any who are truly attempting to balance liberties with public health, no matter the extent to which we would disagree with them on that matter, from those who knew this and persevered with their assault on lady liberty regardless and, by their own outwardly stated logic, for no good reason.

All this was until the final day of writing this book, when New Zealand reinstituted a full national lockdown on account of a single COVID case. The mere fact that this was considered, never mind implemented, is a far more powerful testament to the state of liberty in the Anglosphere than I could ever make.

Already, the policy is defended by those who point to New Zealand's favourable statistical outputs in terms of deaths, which nonetheless remain true.

The practical consideration upon witnessing this is to redirect our efforts away from such jurisdictions, and towards those which have at least created some successful attempt to defend liberty.

Conclusions on Australia and New Zealand

The section's conclusion was stated at its outset, as every good argument should.

Twinned by geography, divergent in policy.

Most obviously, the response in New Zealand has, by its output, outstripped that of Australia whilst avoiding the incursions into liberty which the Australian approach incurred. It would be easy to rant and rail against both, as incursions to liberty on both counts were still made.

However, we must recognise the distance we have travelled from the vaunted days when liberty was valued and conscience the order of the day. The value of New Zealand as an example to the statists and technocrats as a halfway house and test of intent seems unexplored.

More practically than that theoretical use, should you fail in your attempt to advocate for liberty on every other term, resorting to this at the final turn may recover some ground in argument for your favour, especially if your counterparty is tired of the exercise. The final question at the end of the section on Australia, with the new knowledge of the comparison in mind, bears restating: Let the authoritarians answer this – per capita, lives were not saved by their policies. So why on Earth, should they be tolerated any longer?

COVID-19 in India—Delta and Kappa

Freedom is never dear at any price. It is the breath of life. What would a man not pay for living?
—Gandhi

The Second Most Cases in the World

The above statement is true as of the time of writing with India being second only to the U.S. in terms of the number of infections; things may of course change moving forward.

What is immediately noticeable however, is that India suffered less fatalities as a result of infection than the U.S., and also Brazil, which currently tallies fewer infections total.[176]

So, in relative terms of the broadest possible view, India's approach might not deserve the disastrous reputation coverage like it received in the UK garnered it. This is before factoring in the unique challenges of the place when dealing with a pandemic of

---

[176] John Hopkins University. (2021). *Mortality Analyses.* Johns Hopkins Coronavirus Resource Center.
https://coronavirus.jhu.edu/data/mortality

this kind. Prime Minister Modi's approval ratings did drop to a low not seen in many years, though he remains the most popular politician in India.[177]

There are multiple points of optimism to be found for both nation and principle in the approach it took though; let us commit these to posterity here so they are not forgotten.

Repatriation, Self-Reliance and our Saviour *Suo Moto*

One point of the Indian approach to the pandemic which often goes unmentioned was the massive effort mounted to repatriate citizens trapped abroad.

This compared to approaches like the UK, which largely announced travel restrictions and left expatriates and tourists alike to sink or swim, subject to certain exceptions. Called the Vande Bharat mission, its fourth, fifth and sixth phases are ongoing as I write these letters, with a further four from that listed on the government of the Indian website and it has expanded to include not just private airlines, but also Indian permanent residents or 1-year VISA holders wishing to travel elsewhere.[178]

It is by far one of the most ambitious repatriation and evacuation efforts in recorded history, managing to repatriate some 950,000 people in three months,[179] yet outside of India it

---

[177] Miglani, S., & Ghosal, D. (2021, May 18). *PM Modi's rating falls to new low as India reels from COVID-19*. Reuters.
https://www.reuters.com/world/india/pm-modis-rating-falls-india-reels-covid-19-second-wave-2021-05-18/

[178] Ministry of External Affairs. (2021, March 3). *Vande Bharat Mission—List of Flights*. Www.mea.gov.in.
https://www.mea.gov.in/vande-bharat-mission-list-of-flights.htm

[179] *Nearly 9.5 lakh Indians return under Vande Bharat Mission: MEA*. (2020, August 6). Hindustan Times.

seems to have largely gone unnoticed.

As logistically impressive as the operation is, it was subject to criticism, or at least its place in the government's approach was. It was often compared to the plight of internally migrating workers within India itself; national lockdowns were in place at similar times and many states refused to allow travel from one to another in an attempt to contain the virus.

The government was promptly criticised for prioritising a middle class show project over workers at home. Such criticism may be fairly mounted in terms of consequence; Reuters estimates the number of internally migrating workers in India at 100 million,[180] a number which dwarfs the total evacuations from abroad.

The question to unify the fracture must then be twofold—one half efficiency, one half possibility. Beginning with the second, it may have simply been legally or politically impossible to force states to drop the border stringency rules and increased regulations which made life so difficult for migratory workers.

If this is true, though I do not wish to suggest any conclusion, then the question of efficiency is automatically answered—reallocating resources from a possibility to an impossibility would always result in a worse outcome. The difficulty comes if it is found that any level of government could have done something to protect migratory workers and knowingly failed to do so.

My inner voluntarist rails against the consensus that the

---

https://www.hindustantimes.com/india-news/nearly-9-5-lakh-indians-return-under-vande-bharat-mission-mea/story-8MrEitnPhKQaIvR0jc5qCO.html

[180] Nagaraj, R. S., Anuradha. (2020, April 29). *As migrant workers struggle for lockdown aid, India seeks to count them.* Reuters. https://www.reuters.com/article/us-health-coronavirus-india-migrants-fea-idUSKCN22B005

lockdowns and border barriers were necessary at all, but such a vector of criticism may not be politically viable in practice. Aside from the criticism that the government got the ranking of priorities wrong and some tragic difficulties in fulfilling the operational goals, the Vande Bharat mission should stand out on its own merits as a uniquely impressive accomplishment.

The ambition of the Modi government was not sated there however.

It also chose to view the pandemic as an opportunity for a self-reliant India, one which could stand on its own terms and eliminate unfavourable imports. This is not to say that all imports are so, simply those where there would be no other choice.

It chose to go about this in an unusual way however; austerity did not follow, but instead a stimulus package. To the tune of some 20 trillion rupees, or some 10% of India's prior GDP, divided into three phases, though also including previously indicated but yet to execute government actions, such as those made by the Reserve Bank of India through the lockdowns prior to the announcement of the program on May 12th, such as some USD $100bn equivalent in direct liquidity.

The new reforms themselves focused immediately on the construction of infrastructure, support to stressed business, some direct cash injection. Also included were some politically controversial measures, such as the privatisation of the power industry, as pointed out by Sonal Varma.[181]

The government responded by focusing on stimulating the demand-side in it second package on October 12th, making interest free loans available to the various states to boost both capital

---

[181] Ohri, N. (2020, May 17). *Rs 20 Lakh Crore Economic Package With Little Government Spend*. BloombergQuint.
https://www.bloombergquint.com/coronavirus-outbreak/rs-20-lakh-crore-economic-package-with-little-government-spend

expenditure and maintain spending during the imminent celebratory season.

One month later, with a third package the government turned chiefly back to the supply side, spending on green energy, infrastructure and housing. Views on the success of the program vary. Some brand it a mere 'confidence trick' intended as a part political, part placebo project. Others point to corollary changes like the massive rise in Indian electronic exports, though it is worth noting that imports had already fallen relative to exports prior to the announcement of the program.

For the highlight of the approach in India however, we need not look to its legislatures or executive, but its judiciary.

On the 25th of April, the government, by executive decree, ordered the removal of Facebook, Twitter and Instagram posts which it argued were misinformation. A proportion of them just happened to be made by opponents of the government inside and outside Parliament. The case was taken *suo moto* by the Indian Supreme Court, which is to say that it was fast-tracked and heard without prompting by lower courts. On the 30th, the Chief Justice made the following statement about freedom of expression in the country:[182]

> *There should be free flow of information; we should hear voices of citizens. This is a national crisis. There should not be any presumption that the grievances raised on the internet are always false.[...] there should not be any kind of*

---

[182] *No clampdown on grievances; must avoid political bickering: What SC said on COVID crisis.* (2021, April 30). The Times of India. https://timesofindia.indiatimes.com/india/no-clampdown-on-grievances-must-avoid-political-bickering-what-sc-said-on-covid-crisis/articleshow/82330908.cms

clampdown.

The debate which rightly follows is one of which procedure in administrative law best protects liberty.

The Supreme Court in this case doubtless intervened to protect liberty in Indian society and discourse.

However, we have seen, in the constant remanding of cases like *Guedes v BATFE* in the U.S. and its wider imperial status relative to its constitutional mandate that granting courts similar discretion over the cases they hear can lead to disastrous consequences.

However, the power has clearly been deployed to the defence of a valuable cause here, and there are powerful and instinctively familiar arguments concerning access to justice and development of the law at play when invoking these doctrines.

These running that justice is better accessible where the highest court in the land can pursue cases at will, and that the expertise at play is in best place to guide the development of the law to optimal effect.

The best way to reconcile this tension seems then to incorporate the *suo moto* approach as a supplementary power, perhaps in parallel with standard operation where there is spare capacity or set aside entirely as a developmental enterprise.

Neither of these describe the Indian example but seem good ways of incorporating the power.

The key emphasis above all seems to be that, when granting courts discrimination as to the cases they hear, emphasis must be given that this only be used to expand the number or variety of cases heard, rather than a tool like certiorari in the U.S. which has left crucial cases unheard with very real political consequences.

Conclusions on Asia and Australasia

There may seem multiple notable omissions from this chapter. China most obviously, amongst others. The reason for its exclusion is the relative paucity of reliable information on account of censorship in the country, and its location as the origin of the pandemic meaning that others will likely cover it far better. In any case, there was scant liberty to be gained or lost there, rendering it largely outside the scope of this book.

The remainder, I will openly and honestly concede that I did not have time to do sufficient justice to before the time pressure of this book became overwhelming.

Despite the relative shortness of this section however, there are lessons to be learned and conclusions drawn. Firstly, that authoritarian policies regarding COVID-19 have yet to produce the advertised results. The response to this by power-hungry governments has been to either force or demand more authoritarian policies.

Some others have been more moderate, and this should be pointed to as a temporary reprieve or smaller loss. There were still inroads made into liberty in these countries and therefore, no victory.

Many such as Zuby[183] have well made the point about their continual escalation, and the ironic point that, though people comply because they want these measures to stop, their compliance will achieve the exact opposite. The likely conclusion, as I have already alluded to, is that they are not intended to save lives, at least in any thorough sense. They are intended at best to save lives as they are interpreted by boiled down statistics and then ruthlessly compressed by perceived or actual electoral pressure on

---

[183] Zuby. Twitter (2021, July 20).
https://twitter.com/joseph98144676/status/1417411919250706447

the politicians concerned by an electorate selecting on given criteria—thereby triggering Goodhart's law.

Seeing as the sheer number of lives is being selected for, on this charitable view, the technicalities of what qualifies as a life, even if that means destroying its every quality, as governments around the world have so enthusiastically done, will be prioritised.

This is the best possible interpretation.

It also does not seem credible, given that far more moderate governments have produced far better results.

Most importantly, that advocates of liberty should not be closed minded in where we search for it.

There is very often an unfortunate Anglospheric focus to our efforts, when it is precisely that culture which seems to be abandoning liberty and terrified of even the spectre of individual responsibility. More than that, we cannot afford to be closed minded.

Where there is potential for august days, massive economic growth and rampant expansion to come, there we must make our case. To those who would make best use of it and who most keenly feel the need to rapidly develop themselves and the world around them.

It is in these places, to develop in the next 20-50 years, that we must not neglect. I was privileged to, whilst writing this book, have an hour-long conversation with fellow students in the South Asia chapter of Students for Liberty.

Their enthusiasm and erudition made a profound impression on me, far deeper than many at Oxford.

It is that personal note which for me undergirds the necessity of exporting voluntarist ideas to places and cultures where they have room to grow and less of an uphill battle against a welfarist and statist establishment, and populations cowed into submission.

Chapter 7—Conclusions and Final Thoughts

IT FEELS STRANGE to even attempt to write a conclusion on a topic which is far from concluded.

The implications of COVID-19 will likely haunt every facet of our lives for years to come. Yet, closing on a final recapitulation remains an effective authorial style, so attempted it must be.

Likely incoming and entrenched travel restrictions will affect even those from nations which took an approach which preserved liberties, as discussed in the cases of Sweden and Switzerland.

Across the remainder of Europe, vaccine passports, the enshrinement of technocracy, the expansion of the state's margin of appreciation in medical matters and a clear default to supranationalism when push comes to shove, will endanger any remnant of liberty left on the very continent which gave birth to the modern conception of it.

In America, debates over mask mandates in schools still rage and there seems at least some hope that the Republican Party may run a candidate such as Governor DeSantis who would oppose such policies, though whether any meaningful opposition can be mounted before the Biden administration does its worst is doubtful.

The UK's handling of the crisis has been temperamental at best and self-destructive at worst from beginning to end, with no notable opposition to defend liberty from the predations of the First Johnson Ministry.

Whilst this work remains regrettably incomplete as a survey of the world's responses to COVID-19, the approaches by nations in Asia and Australasia perhaps make the best case and goal for where those who care about freedom should focus their goals. Australia's results manifestly show that authoritarian approaches do not deliver on their results; to explicitly state it again, this is because they are not created out of a desire to protect people, but out of a wish to more thoroughly dominate those people through the Leviathan.

The efficiency of the Japanese approach stands out, despite its surrounding controversies and the lack of any deontological protections to liberty. Whilst New Zealand stands out in consequential regards as a halfway compromise to aim for given no other alternative, it is just that, a compromise, with most recent actions shutting down the nation for one case utterly unworkable elsewhere, never mind nightmarish.

India has doubtless been rocked by the virus, though there are reasons to look at its approach positively in contrast to the uniformly negative coverage it seems to have been given in the West.

Perhaps the most immediate positive is that the statist response to voluntarists that liberty is best guarded by the state is now well and truly bankrupted. Governments all over the world have proven that liberty as a right, or series of rights, means nothing to them if it is even perceived to get in their way, never mind the actuality.

The resulting realisation, that the defence of liberty is the responsibility of each and every individual, is weighty.

Dostoyevsky put it better than I ever could: 'Every one is really responsible to all men for all men and for everything.' As far as it manifests as a personal responsibility though, there seems to be an appeal, at least to the younger generation, as the success of persons like Professor Peterson manifestly demonstrates.

The key then, is to show those who can be convinced that negative liberty is a personal responsibility as much as positive 'liberty' is, if not more so.

Whilst this is less immediately obvious due to the nature of the rights under each category, the prevailing zeitgeist has rendered the political landscape such that those wishing to defend traditional, consistent, negative liberty, must defend it in every instance—they must defend everyone else's right to life, freedom, bodily autonomy and property, against those individuals who would infringe it and governments corrupted by lying ideologues, possessed by false gods.

Above all, these events have shown that every opportunity to defend and advance liberty by individuals in their own life and in their own praxis must be taken.

Those sworn by Constitution to defend it cannot be trusted—Biden recently supported legislation which even he doubted the constitutionality of, seemingly because he owes allegiance to his own whims more than the document which he swore to defend upon taking office, in front of millions of witnesses.

Any Constitution is only as good as it is taken to be by actions, either in minded reverence of those taking action, or the stringent defence of those reacting.

In either case, the document itself is little more than a reflection, encapsulation and manifesto of its undergirding principles.

In summary, magic napkins do not give you your rights, your

humanity does, and any other approach is defeasible both at pure logic and by the facts staring us in the face.

Others, such as those in the UK with no fixed and codified constitution, must be faced with overwhelming incentive not to further infringe and corresponding incentive to advance. This must be cultivated by cultural action which inculcates liberty's value, which has been ongoing with varying degrees of success.

If you take nothing else from this book, that is it.

Change your own life to defend the liberties in it, defend those of others where you can, and spread that message as far and wide as possible.

If you were looking for a call to action, for a message to rally around, for proof that young people are willing to risk their future to publicly defend freedom, this is it.

Should we, you and I fail to do so, I point to the victims of freedom's demise.

More than you or I, it is those to come, who cannot consent or defend themselves, who will be the victims of this precedent and policies.

So, in defence of the defenceless, onwards.

Pax Libertas.